Voices from the Center of the World

Contemporary Poets of Ecuador

For Katherine M. Hedeen
and Víctor Rodríguez Núñez

CONTENTS

FOREWORD

At the height of her prodigious powers, Margaret Randall has crowned a lifelong commitment to art and activism with an astounding body of work written in the last ten years. In addition to powerful volumes of poetry, among them *Time's Language: Selected Poems 1959-2018* (2018) and *Against Atrocity* (2019), Randall unites social memoir, biography, and the critical account, in such books as *Che on My Mind* (2013), *Haydée Santamaría, Cuban Revolutionary: She Led by Transgression* (2015), and *Exporting Revolution: Cuba's Global Solidarity* (2017). She continues to extend the foundational work first begun with the literary journal *El Corno Emplumado* by devoting energies to the translation and advocacy of poetry from the Americas.

In *Voices from the Center of the World*, Randall has assembled a constellation of 25 poets born in Ecuador between 1926 and 1993. The sampling begins with avant-garde pioneer Jorgenrique Adoum (1926-2009), whose writings were at the front lines of a modernist formation that included such poets as César Dávila Andrade (1918-1967, who lived and worked largely in Caracas, Venezuela), and painters Oswaldo Guayasamin and Camilo Egas (who lived in New York and taught at the New School for Social Research). Adoum's poetry continued to cast an influence with its deeply interior properties, its cascade of harrowing voices that question human existence in the subjugations of underdevelopment, especially as connected to the historical aftermath and present realities of internal and external colonialism, with its violent inequalities and brutally uneven social distributions. Like other intellectuals in Latin America in relation to the modern State, Adoum viewed collective identity not as something definable or immutable, determined by historical antecedent, but as the accumulation of features in a group self-portrait, and as a form of collage.[1] In a national imagination suspended between "colonial continuity" and "historical continuity," a generative self-awareness drives poetry from Ecuador, as elsewhere in Latin America, between regional description and international idioms. Poetry at this juncture draws from pre-conquest, colonial, modern, and contemporary accounts; it serves as a form of social memory enlivened by language and iconographies connected to literary sources, the popular imagination, and the changing hue of everyday struggles; it speaks in the accents of exuberance and hesitation.

The range of forms and meanings in this collection confirm a proclivity to reimagine the natural landscape and urban geographies of the present. Distinct voices nonetheless point back to twentieth-century currents that advocated for a poem's intellectual vitality, artistic experimentation, and a commitment to a plural national culture. Emerging from a regard for how newness enters the world is the exciting work of women authors born between 1950 and 1958—Sara Vanegas (1950), Catalina Sojos (1951), Maritza Cino Alvear (1957), Carmen Váscones (1958)—and of more recent poets Julia Erazo (1972) and Carlos Vallejo (1973). Writing in the Kichwa language, Ariruma Kowii (1961) and Lucila Lema (1974) serve as custodians of indigenous knowledge and imaginations, at once political, historical, and ancestral. Randall relates that in contemporary Ecuador, especially in the region around Esmeraldas, photographers, artists, choreographers, and poets, including Antonio Preciado (1941), have been preserving and honoring the

---

1. Jorge Enrique Adoum, *Ecuador: señas particulares* (Quito: Edición Eskeletra Editorial, 2000), p 24. "Ante todo, la identidad colectiva no es algo definido e inmutable, conformado por los siglos anteriores a nosotros, que hubiéramos recibido como una instantánea del pasado, menos aún como un tatuaje que no podemos borrar, sino que se va haciendo, como un autorretrato, por acumulación de rasgos o como un collage."

legacies of slavery and the contribution of Afro-Ecuadorians to contemporary culture.

These "Voices from the Center of the World" are inflected with the effects of omens and effigies, with the sites of pyramids and tribunals, and with the footprints of existence and of "that which survives obscurity" (Catalina Sojos). Margaret Randall's selection and translations are alert to the edges and cadences of an individual idiom, to the plural alignments with the long view of history, and to consciousness of the country's literary dynamism. This volume reverberates with living stones and magnetic energies—with humanity, as Julia Erazo writes, in "the embrace / of new liquids and ancient voices."

—Roberto Tejada, Ph.D.
Distinguished Professor of English and
Creative Writing, University of Houston

PROLOGUE

Octavio Paz once wrote: "There's no Argentinian or Mexican or Venezuelan poetry, only Latin American poetry or, more precisely, a Latin American tradition and style. The national histories of our literature are as artificial as our political borders."[1] I disagree. While I consider Paz himself a great poet, with a definite Mexican essence, I would have challenged him—would challenge anyone—to deny that every country has its own culture, one that produces a national voice in many individual registers.

Borders are arbitrary and fictitious when drawn by colonialism, or when splitting the homelands of indigenous peoples. But 500 years necessarily nurture unique histories, ways of using language, disparate offerings of idiom and voice. This is true for Spanish or Portuguese, Guaraní, French, English, Mayan, Quechua, Mapuche, among the many other languages of the Americas. Who, having read Mexican poetry, can remain oblivious to a powerful precolonial presence or to that nation's love/hate relationship with its bully neighbor to the North? Who reads Argentinian or Uruguayan poets without catching a whiff of Rioplatense irony or being touched by the ghosts of a generation of disappeared? In Paraguay, the only Latin American country with two official languages, Guaraní is a strong linguistic presence. Peruvian and Bolivian poetry exude an Andean sobriety. Nicaragua is a nation of poets, its verse often richly familiar and conversational. Cubans are islanders, balanced between the public and private through sixty years of decisive social change; its poetry, over the past several decades at least, very often reflects an embrace or rejection of that change. It would be absurd to claim that Bolivia, a country

---

1. Quoted in *La Estafeta del Viento* by Edwin Madrid (Visor Libros, Madrid, 2007), p. 20.

with no exit to the sea, produces the same sort of poetry as Cuba, an island surrounded by water. Chile, Brazil, Ecuador: each Latin American nation has its idiosyncrasies, palpable in the voices of its poets. As Cuban poet Víctor Rodríguez Núñez says: "I don't always write about Cuba, but I always write from Cuba."

Edwin Madrid, in his in-depth prologue to the anthology of Ecuadoran poetry he published with Visor in 2007, asks: "Is there such a thing as Ecuadoran poetry? Because if we look at literature's map, we find Gabriel García Márquez to the north and the poet César Vallejo to the south. And what runs through Ecuadoran territory is an imaginary line. Ecuador, in the concert of universal literature, isn't even a written line but an imaginary one, something so inexistent and imaginary that it is represented by a line of zeros: Latitude 0° 0″ 0′. Nevertheless, generation after generation Ecuador's poets offer us freer readings of the world."[2] I believe that line, with its very imaginary nature, is precisely one of the strongest indicators of the uniqueness of the country's poetry.

This book does not pretend to be an anthology. Rather, it is a sampling: of the poetry I brought back with me after attending the *Poesía Paralelo Cero 2019* festival and selected as I read the work of other Ecuadoran poets. I first encountered the poetry of Ecuador in the 1960s when I co-founded and co-edited *El Corno Emplumado / The Plumed Horn* out of Mexico City. In our sixth issue (April 1963), the journal published a small anthology of Ecuadoran poems, and continued to keep in touch with writers and artists from that country. Back then, we particularly connected with the Tzantzicos, two of whom so many years later appear here. In the same decade we got to know Miguel Donoso Pareja, who had been granted political asylum in Mexico. As I read for this book, I couldn't help but notice how many of

---

2. Idem., p. 18.

Ecuador's more recent poets got their start at the writing workshops he conducted after he was able to return from exile.

Although I would rather call this a sampling than an anthology, I did employ certain criteria to its makeup. Rather than try to include Ecuador's many iconic poets, I decided to represent them only by Jorgenrique Adoum, and then privilege more recent poets unknown to date in the United States but who, aside from their own work, conformed important literary groups or mentored generations of younger writers. I have also wanted to showcase women and indigenous writers, two categories traditionally absent from most selections. And I left room at the end for at least a few new voices I believe we may hear from in the future.

I coincide with many in my belief that the greatest of all Ecuadoran poets is Jorgenrique Adoum. He may be one of the greatest Latin American poets of our era, and it is appalling that a major body of his work has not been available in English translation until now.[3] It seemed logical to begin this selection with him. Despite the size limitation, a range of cities and poetic voices are represented. Donoso Pareja's poem to his mother is heavy with the pain of exile, something common to so many who were forced to flee the Latin American dictatorships of the 1970s and 80s. Estrella evokes the living force of the volcano that towers above Quito. Preciado's poems vibrate with the African culture that can still be so powerfully felt in his native Esmeraldas. Arias makes words themselves the protagonist in one of his poems.

Iza, Vanegas, Sojos, Alvear, Váscones, Quevedo, Erazo, and Blum are only some of the women whose voices emerged with the rise of feminism during the second half

---

3. This lack has finally been remedied by Katherine M. Hedeen and Víctor Rodríguez Núñez's masterful translation of three of Adoum's books combined in a single volume: *Prepoems in PostSpanish and Other Poems* (Action Books, 2020).

of the twentieth century; each with its own character and timbre. Palacios gives us her unique take on haiku, a verse form that has engaged almost every Ecuadoran poet at one time or another. Madrid writes about the Galápagos Islands, admitting that he has never been to them even as he acknowledges their powerful claim on Ecuador's identity. Oquendo, in his poem about his grandparents, references deeply-rooted Quiteño tradition. Carlos Vallejo's voice falls between the surreal and experimental. Bravo's poem about a woman found beaten-up and dead in a swimming pool is a commentary on the classism and crass hypocrisy so prevalent in all our societies.

I also wanted to be sure to include Ecuador's indigenous poets; the poetry world, to its credit, is finally beginning to pay attention to the many living indigenous literatures. In their poems presented in Kichwa (the dialect of Quechua that is spoken in Ecuador and Colombia), Spanish, and English translation, Kowii and Lema address issues as pertinent today as they were to their ancestors, bringing their world vision into focus for the reader. The selection ends with poets born after 1950, several of them in the 1990s. Grijalva, Gordillo and Suárez Proaño represent the youngest generation, whose work shows promise today and will reach maturity in the years to come.

Ecuador is situated on the equator, the center of the world as its people are quick to point out. After my visit (not my first to the country), I would suggest that this geographical placement carries with it a certain magnetic energy, and that this magnetic energy is palpable. I'm not talking about some esoteric power field but the science that explains why whirlpools spin in opposite directions on either side of a latitudinal parallel. I venture to say this phenomenon claims an invisible—sometimes visible—presence in the consciousness of many of the country's poets.

Margaret Randall
Spring 2019

Voices from the Center of the World

Contemporary Poets of Ecuador

JORGENRIQUE ADOUM
(1926-2009)

In my opinion Ecuador's most original and powerful poet, I have chosen Adoum to open this selection of his country's poetry. Previously known as Jorge Enrique Adoum, he began combining his two given names towards the end of his life. Adoum was born in Ambato. He held a number of positions in international organizations, visiting Egypt, India, Japan and Israel under the auspices of the United Nations, working in French radio and television, reading for that country's Gallimard Publishers in the 1960s, and collaborating closely with Cuba's Casa de las Américas from that decade until his death. One of his books was awarded the first poetry prize Casa gave. Pablo Neruda said of Adoum: "Ecuador has the greatest poet in [Latin] America."

Xavier Oquendo has written of him: "Without doubt he is the most influential poet of the second half of the twentieth century. Because of his important innovations in language and structure, he is considered our most international and complete (he wrote in all genres with the same quality and seeming effortlessness). In terms of morphology and semantics, Adoum was responsible for the most truly vanguardist poetry of his generation. [But] because he was Pablo Neruda's secretary, myopic critics accused him of writing in the shadow of *Canto General* . . ." Edwin Madrid points out, however, that it was while working for Neruda that Adoum got to know Nicolás Guillén Miguel Ángel Asturias, Rafael Alberto, Violeta Parra." In other words, some of the greatest creative minds of his time. The experience undoubtedly gave him access to a rich and powerful world. Adoum also wrote novels, essay, and theater. Katherine M. Hedeen and Víctor Rodríguez Núñez have brilliantly translated three of his most important collections into English, making his work available here for the first time.

Among his poetry collections are: *Ecuador amargo* (1949), *Carta para Alejandra* (1952), *Los cuadernos de la tierra: I. Los orígenes, II. El enemigo y la mañana* (1952), *Notas del hijo pródigo* (1953), *Relato del extranjero* (1955), *Los cuadernos de la Tierra: III. Dios Trajo la Sombra* (1959), *Los cuadernos de la tierra: IV. El dorado y las ocupaciones nocturnas* (1961), *Informe personal sobre la situación* (1975), *No son todos los que están* (1979), and *Poesía viva del Ecuador* (1990).

HISTORIA

Al comienzo, la patria
fue una gran página en blanco:
la arena, el mar, la superficie,
la sombra verde, la tinta
con que manchó el invierno la sabana.
Pero de pronto, sin que nada
pudiera detenerlo, hay un hombre
conduciendo a su familia por los márgenes,
entra, cae y escala hasta el renglón
ecuatorial buscando vida.
Yo vengo desde allí: desayuné con ellos
en la primera mañana de mi pueblo,
construimos sembríos contra el hambre,
un río de cereal llevamos a la harina
y supimos las leyes del agua y de la luna.

De la segunda página hasta hoy día
no hay sino violencia. Desde
el segundo día no hubo día
en que no nos robaran la casa
y el maíz y ocuparan la tierra
que amé como a una isla de ternura.

Pero mañana (mucho antes
de lo que habíamos pensado)

echaré al invasor y llamaré a mi hermano
e iremos juntos hasta la geografía
—el dulce arroz, la recua del petróleo—
y le diré: Señora, buenos días,
aquí estamos después de tantos siglos
a cobrar juntas todas las gavillas,
a contar si están justos los quilates
y a saber cuánta tierra nos queda todavía.

HISTORY

In the beginning, the nation
was a great white page:
sand, sea, surface,
green shadow, ink
winter staining the sheet.
But suddenly, as if nothing
could stop him, there is a man
leading his family along the edges,
he enters, falls and climbs
to the equator searching for life.
I come from that place: ate breakfast with them
on my people's first morning,
we planted fields against hunger,
shaped wheat into a river of cereal
and knew the laws of water and the moon.

From page two until the present
there is nothing but violence. From
the second day there wasn't one
when they didn't rob our homes
and corn and occupy this earth
I loved like an island of tenderness.

But tomorrow (long before
we thought possible)
I will vanquish the invader, call my brother
and together we will find geography
—sweet rice, petroleum's flock—
and I will say: Good day, Madam,
here we are after so many centuries
ready to gather all the sparrows,
make sure they weigh what they should
and learn how much land we have left.

YO ME FUI CON TU NOMBRE POR LA TIERRA

Nadie sabe en dónde queda mi país, lo buscan
entristeciéndose de miopía: no puede ser,
tan pequeño ¿y es tanta su desgarradura,
tanto su terremoto, tanta tortura
militar, más trópico que el trópico?

                                        Tampoco
lo sé yo, yo que lo amo a pesar de mis jueces
(la Corte se reúne en el café las tardes,
y ni un testigo sino mi taza que pagaron
una vez). Y, condenado a muerte en su dulce
calabozo, abro los ojos de vez en cuando,
lo veo igual y le pregunto: ¿Qué siglo
será hoy, dónde se esconde el corazón
para hacerme doler?

                         Si de la tierra
no te quedara amar sino el paisaje, si solamente
te faltara la espalda agresiva de la luz.
Pero no es ése el caso. Sucede que no estoy
orgulloso de mi aldea, ni de su río, el único
que sigue siendo el mismo bañándote en él cien veces,
ni de la cometa que enarbola el polvo
en el mercado. No me dejan estarlo, no me han dejado
nunca unos señores compatriotas, cincuenta
años en la misma esquina calculando
los mismos asuntos importantes —el mundo
sólo va de su bolsillo a su bragueta— y ven
pasar el tren y no lo toman, ven acercarse
el día pero se acuestan, ven la vida pasar
pero regresan y animal, voluntariosísimamente
se amarran por el cuello al palo de la iglesia.

Debo estar orgulloso, ¿de qué si la ternura
solteronas de ambos sexos me robaron en la infancia,
aprovechando que no estuve? ¿Y lo demás, cuando
indagan si es aún una colonia pobrecita,
con la cabeza a un lado, mientras le abren
la blusa democráticamente? ¿Qué puedo
contestar si ven la fecha de hoy y notan
que vive el encomendero todavía en su fósil,
si me miran llevando un indio de la mano,

aterido de patrón y tiempo, intacto en la obediente
piedra, estatua para adentro, con que lo
llenaron?
        Ah si fuera dable por un día

limpiar el amor de todo cuanto es cierto,
como cuando nos toca los párpados el delirio.
Porque a veces no es posible tolerar a la madre
con sus cosas.
        Quisiera entonces que no encuentren

la lupa, que no miren de cerca lo difícil, eso
no nuestro, tan desprecio, tan asco. Pero insisten
y como soy patriota digo: "Sucede que los Incas".

En dónde queda, di, di qué le hicieron.

I Carried Your Name Around the World

No one knows where my country is, they look
for it saddened by their myopia: it shouldn't be
so small, and could it be so shattered,
so earthquake, so military torture,
more tropical than the tropics?
                                        I don't know
either, I who love it in spite of my judges
(Court is in session each afternoon at the café,
without a single witness except the single cup
they paid for). And condemned to death
in its sweet dungeon, once in a while I open my eyes,
it looks the same and I ask it: What century
is it now, where has it hidden its heart
to cause me such pain?
                                        If earth
didn't let you love the landscape, if only
you lacked the light's brilliant backdrop.
But that isn't it. The truth is, I'm not
proud of my village, nor its river, the only thing
still the same although I bathe in it a hundred times,
nor am I proud of the comet that raises dust
in the marketplace. They won't let me be proud, they've
never let me, my countrymen, fifty years
on the same corner pondering
the same auspicious events —the world
only exists from their pocket to their fly— and they
watch the train go by and don't take it, see day
approach but go to bed, witness life pass
but return and, like animals, so willingly
tie their necks to religion's post.

I should be proud, of what, if old maids
of both sexes stole my infant tenderness,
taking advantage of my absence?
And the rest of it, when they ask
with downcast eyes if it's
still a poor colony, even as they
unbutton its blouse democratically? What
can I say if they notice today's date and understand
the messenger still lives in his fossil,
if they see me leading an Indian by the hand,
rigid with master and time, silent
in obedient stone, statue inside and out,
what did they fill him with?

       Ah, even for a day
if we were able to cleanse love of all that is true,
like when delirium brushes our eyelids.
Because sometimes it isn't possible to tolerate
the mother and her things.

      That's when I wish
they would lose the magnifying glass,
wouldn't scrutinize what is difficult
or doesn't belong to us, such scorn, such disgust.
But they insist and I'm a patriot so I say: "It was the Inca."

Where they still exist, tell, tell what they did to them.

MIGUEL DONOSO PAREJA
(1931-2015)

Born in Guayaquil into a family of writers, Donoso Pareja was active with other poets and writers of his generation from the early 1950s on. In 1962 he joined Ecuador's Communist Party, beginning a life of political activism which, in turn, led to his being accused of terrorism. In July 1963, Ramón Castro Jijón took dictatorial power and Donoso Pareja was forced underground. He came out of hiding one day to take two of his daughters to the movies, was discovered, captured and spent the following ten months in prison without a trial. He was finally able to seek refuge in Mexico, where he brought his family, a few at a time, and lived until 1981 when he decided to return to his native land. In 1987 he was elected president of the Casa de la Cultura Ecuatoriana in the province of Guayas and moved permanently to Guayaquil. His later years were plagued by his struggle with Parkinson's. Donoso Pareja's poems included here reflect the anguish of exile experienced by so many Latin American poets who were politically active during the 1960s through '80s.

Among Donoso Pareja's poetry collections are: *La mutación del hombre* (1957), *Las raíces del hombre* (1958), *Los invencibles* (1963), *Primera canción del exiliado* (1966, bilingual edition), *Cantos para celebrar una muerte* (1977), *Última canción del exiliado* (1994), and *Adagio en G mayor para una letra difunta* (2002).

REGRESO

a mi Madre

Estamos hoy muy cerca y sin embargo lejos.
En mis grises designios de amargas latitudes
fui dejando tus besos sepultados de olvido.
Y me he quedado solo,
mirando la verticalidad pretérita
de un poste desplomado,
o la horizontalidad en crisis de los senos
de una moza olvidada.
Y como dos extraños,
sin besos y palabras hermosas,
separando un abismo nuestro amor verdadero,
voy alargándome hacia ti
por el cordón umbilical de una mirada perdida,
como este puerto mío que se alarga en su ansiedad de océano
vengo a rogar tu amor y a dejar mi promesa
por un mejor mañana.

Tengo la sal de mi naufragio, tengo
una piedra en el alma y en los ojos
una ansiedad preñada de caminos,
una implacable sed; en las entrañas
y sobre el corazón y en el cerebro
tengo el azúcar de la tierra porque tú me la has dado.

Hay tantas cosas.
Tantas verdades que se escapan a los ojos
porque un beso nos amarra, en la distancia, la mirada.
Tantas verdades que se niegan,
porque hay un mar que llora abrazado del alma,
… y un doler
y una borrachera en la que vivo un mundo inaccesible,
inalcanzable,
como la ingenua sonrisa de una niña loca.

Madre hoy vengo a ti angustiado.
Con la angustia de un libro maltratado por un torpe
o un hombre esperando en una esquina
a la mujer de otro.
O el que escucha en la sala de una clínica,
su alimentado semen en el llanto de un hijo.

Vengo tímido y vengo avergonzado.
Con la timidez y la vergüenza de una sonrisa sin dientes
o un joven masturbándose.
Con la vergüenza de una niña desnuda
por primera vez ante los ojos de un hombre.
Con la vergüenza de un libro en la vitrina
que no es comprado nunca.
Vengo llorando.
Dejando al viento mis lágrimas de hijo
para que se unan al inmenso sistema de tu tanto
formado por tus lágrimas de madre.

Estarás orgullosa porque seré otro hombre
y he matado mi triste soledad y mi llanto
y ahora son las distancias y las acciones buenas
y aunque estamos muy cerca y sin embargo lejos
yo haré que esta acidez se convierta en dulzura
y de esta despedida sin viaje volveremos
para darnos un beso cuando estemos de vuelta.

RETURN

to my Mother

Today we are so close yet so far from each other.
On my gray journeys to bitter latitudes
I left your kisses buried in oblivion.
I remain alone,
gazing at the vertical history
of a fallen post
or your breasts in the horizontal crisis
of an abandoned boy.
And like two strangers,
with neither kisses nor beautiful words
separating the vast expanse of our love
I leave, wandering toward you
along the umbilical cord of a lost look,
like this port of mine that moves off on its ocean of anxiety
I come to plea for your love and promise you
a better tomorrow.

I taste the salt of my shipwreck, there is
a stone in my soul and in my eyes
the fraught tension of this passage,
insatiable thirst; in my gut
and heart and mind I hold
the sweetness of my land, your legacy.

There is so much.
So many truths that escape my eyes
because we are joined by a kiss, in the distance, by a look.
So many truths denied,
for there is a sea that cries embracing my soul,
. . . and pain
and the drunkenness in which I exist in an inaccessible

world,
unreachable,
like the innocent smile of a crazy little girl.

Mother today I come to you in anguish.
The anguish of a book tossed aside,
a man waiting on a corner
for another man's wife.
Or one who in a clinic hears
his fortified semen in the cry of his son.

I come to you hesitant and humiliated.
With the fear and shame of a toothless smile
or young boy masturbating.
The shame of a naked young girl
standing before a man for the first time.
With the shame of the book in the window
no one ever buys.
I come in tears
and deposit my tears of a son in the wind
that they may join the immense system of everything
created by your mother's weeping.

You will be proud because I will be someone else.
I have killed my sad loneliness and weeping
and now there are distances and good deeds
and although we are close yet far away
I will turn this bitterness to sweet
and from this motionless goodbye we will return
to kiss one another when we are home again.

ULISES ESTRELLA
(1939-2014)

Ulises Estrella was one of the founders of the Tzántzicos in 1961. Tzánzicos, which means shrunken heads and refers to the reduction of human heads practiced in the past by several indigenous cultures, was part of a world-wide independent artistic renaissance that surged throughout the 1960s and included the Nadaistas in Colombia, Techo de la Ballena in Venezuela, El Corno Emplumado in Mexico, Hungryalists in India and similar groups across the globe, creating a powerful web of rebellious creative nonconformists. Estrella founded and for many years directed Ecuador's National Cinema. He was a longtime cultural reference in his country.

Among Estrella's poetry collections are: *Clamor* (1962), *Ombligo del mundo* (1966), *Convulsionario* (1974), *Aguja que rompe el tiempo* (1980), *Fuera del juego* (1983), *Sesenta poemas* (1984), *Interiores* (1986), *Furtivos, poemas furtivos* (1988), *Peatón de Quito* (1992), *Digo mundo* (2001), and *Contrafactual* (2014). He also wrote essay and theater, and a memoir, *Memoria incandescente*, came out in 2003.

OLOR DE SANTIDAD

MariAna
es
y no es

Aparece, casi estática,
mitad
ángel
con su pecho apretado.

Oliendo
su ciudad,
queriendo
que vengan los temblores
para empezar a comprender
sin cilicios
sin treguas,
abrazando a los humanos,
MariAna,
en su quebradura
trastabillando
en las calles,
viviendo
en la quebrada,
cediendo
su sangre a los diez mil.
Buscando
convertir
en música
el estrépito.

SAINTHOOD'S SCENT

MariAna
is
and isn't

She appears, almost motionless,
half
angel
clasping her breast.

Smelling
her city,
wanting
the earth's tremors to come
so with neither hair shirt
nor ceasefire
she may begin to understand,
embracing humans,
stumbling through the streets
in her rupture
MariAna,
living
in the gorge,
ceding
her blood to the ten thousand.
Looking
to turn
the din
to music.

PIEDRAS VIVAS

Si vinieron del Volcán
estas piedras
trajeron el Fuego

del contorno
al centro,
muy adentro
están fortificadas

desde los bordes
llaman a las caricias,
a descubrir los impulsos
apenas con el tacto
de quienes quieran descubrir
las fiebres internas.

Si fueron expulsadas
desde el fondo de la tierra
son quiteñas sustancias,
Piedras Vivas
que acompasan
los ritmos antagónicos
de nuestros corazones.

Semejantes a cabezas humanas
podrían haber salido de la Caverna
en busca de espacios donde apoyarse.

LIVING STONES

If they came from the Volcano
these stones
brought Fire

from circumference
to center,
deep inside
they are powerful

at their edges,
calling on caresses
to discover desire
with the simple touch of those
who search for hidden flame.

If they were expelled
from the depths of the earth
their substance belongs to Quito,
Living Stones
in step with
the antagonistic rhythms
of our hearts.

Like human heads
they might have emerged from the Cave
looking for a place to rest.

ANTONIO PRECIADO
(1941-)

Antonio Preciado was born in the northwestern port city of Esmeraldas, a place rich in the tragic and combative history of slavery and proud of its black heritage which is vibrantly preserved in music, dance and the spoken word. Preciado's father abandoned the family when his son was very young, leaving his mother to fend for herself and five children. He grew up in a shack without electricity or other modern conveniences. From an early age he sold lottery tickets and newspapers to help support his family. It was with great sacrifice that the future poet was able to finish primary, middle and high school in his city of origin, and travel to Quito where he earned degrees in Political Science and Economics. He has been a university professor, his country's Minister of Culture, and has represented Ecuador as its ambassador to Nicaragua. Preciado's poetry reflects his black roots; he credits his maternal grandmother, Francisca, with teaching him about the traditions of his ancestors. When he was older, he joined the Communist Party, convinced that the ideas of Marx and Lenin signaled the surest road to social justice.

Among Preciado's poetry collections are: *Jolgorio* (1961), *Este hombre y su planeta* (1965), *Más allá de los muertos* (1966), *Siete veces la vida* (1967), *Tal como somos* (1969), *De sol a sol* (1979), *Poema húmedo* (2981), *Espantapájaros* (1982), *De ahora en adelante* (1993), *De boca en boca* (2005), and *De par en par* (2005)

ANIMA PRIMERA

Todas las noches salgo
a hablar con los fantasmas.
Todos llegan a tiempo con el viento
agitando sus nombres
en una multitud desesperada.

¡Ah!
Juana la lavandera
solo anda en noches claras.
Siempre me llega en lunas,
lunas,
lunas,
chapoteando el agua.

Ved que me lavan los ojos,
que me enjuagan la palabra
veintiún manos azucenas,
con agua de nueve charcas.

Ángel, ¿quién enjabonó
trece veces tus dos alas?
¿Entiendes, Dios, la blancura
de tu espléndida garnacha?

¡Guardián del noveno cielo,
llueve una lluvia de nácar,
porque Juana ensangrentó
una punta de su sábana!

FIRST SOUL

Every night I go out
to speak with ghosts.
All show up on time, wind
rustling their names
in anxious multitude.

Ah!
Juana the washerwoman
only comes on clear nights.
She always arrives with the moon,
the moon,
the moon,
sloshing about in water.

Watch as they bathe my eyes,
twenty-one lily hands
rinsing my word
in the water of nine pools

Angel, who thirteen times
lathered up your two wings?
God, do you understand the clarity
of your splendid grape?

Guardian of the ninth heaven,
a mother of pearl rain falls,
because Juana bloodied
the edge of the sheet!

POEMA PARA EL MURO DE UNA CÁRCEL

Digo falda insumisa,
dignidad de una espina,
luna nueva;
pero digo también que todavía
tienen a flor de piel la trampa puesta
paraególatra sandalia perseguida;
yo digo que, en el fondo de la herida,
aún sigue Ángela Davis prisionera,
Ángela y los demás,
la muchedumbre
que, así como quien dice el mar de cerca,
aquí conmigo se agiganta,
ruge,
agita enardecida este poema,
vuelca la copa
y el veneno huye
y se bebe a sí mismo
y se envenena;
pisa en la vida
y el cadalso se hunde
en tanto que el verdugo desespera
porque tras otras fábulas descubre
que se le están virando las sentencias,
y se dice otro adiós mientras escurre
el lazo de la horca
entre sus propias piernas.

POEM FOR A PRISON WALL

Rebellious skirt, I say,
dignity of bone,
new moon;
but I also say her skin
still booby trapped when the narcissist's shoe
hunted her down;
I say, in the depth of the wound,
Angela Davis remains a prisoner,
Angela and the others,
survivors
who, like the nearby sea says,
grow beside me,
become huge, roar,
compel this poem to fire,
overturn the cup
and the poison flees
and drinks itself
and dies;
trampling life
the gallows disappear
as the hangman becomes desperate
because behind other fables he discovers
the verdicts turning upon themselves,
and he utters another goodbye
as the noose slips
between his own legs.

ANA MARÍA IZA
(1941-2016)

Ana María Iza was one of the earliest female voices to emerge among the past century's poets in Ecuador, signaling the beginnings of an explicitly feminist consciousness in that country. Born in Quito, she studied journalism, but interrupted her studies to attend a music conservatory and had success in that field as well. Throughout the last decades of the 20th century, Iza won almost every important poetry prize her country had to offer. Ecuador's great writers wrote glowingly of her, although she herself preferred to labor quietly, producing a strong body of work punctuated by flashes of irony. She was an example for the women poets who followed her: Sonia Manzano, Catalina Sojos, Sara Vanegas, Maritza Cino Alvear, Carmen Váscones, Ana Cecilia Blum, and Julia Erazo, among others. Xavier Oquendo has written of Iza: "Her poetry says so much it bleeds."

Among her poetry collections are: *Pedazo de nada* (1961), *Los cajones del insomnio* (1967), *Puertas inútiles* (1968), *Heredarás el viento* (1974), *Fiel al humo* (1986), *Reflejo del sol sobre las piedras* (1987), *Papeles asustados* (1994), and *Herrumbre persistente* (1995).

JOSÉ

a José V. Riccio L.
(duerme...)

Las compañeras del tercero "E"
anotaban las citas:
X y Y en La Pradera
Z y C en el cinema
J y A en el cementerio

Tú José
Yo Ana
¿Te parecen crueles José las compañeras..?
Cruel la vida crudísima certera

Al jardín del olvido te seguía
mi ramito uniformado de tristeza

Han pasado más siglos que en la Historia
Crecimos
Reciclamos
Círculos círculos círculos
hasta que se abra el suelo

Tú el primer beso
El primer extramuro

Tu piel se hizo ceniza
pero no tu verdad

José
la vida no te alcanzó a matar

Mi boca discípula de tu boca
Te fuiste
sin saber esa Buena Noticia

En las nieves mayúsculas
apareció tu beso
me lavó el rostro
me acarició el cabello

Me dió la mano

Me echó a andar

JOSÉ

to José V. Riccio L.
(sleep...)

The women in Three "E"
kept notes of the meetings:
X and Y at La Pradera
Z y C at the movies
J and A in the cemetery

You, José
Me, Ana
¿Do the women seem cruel to you, José...?
Does life seem cruel, brutal, certain?

My uniformed sprig of sadness
followed you to the garden of oblivion

More than History's centuries have passed
We grow
We recycle ourselves
Circles circles circles
until earth opens

You my first kiss
First otherness

Your skin turned to ashes
but not your truth

José
life wasn't able to kill you

My mouth was your mouth's disciple
You left
without hearing the Good News

Your kiss appeared
in capital letters in the snow
it washed my face
caressed my hair

Gave me its hand

Enabled me to walk

LOBO AZUL

No quise detenerte
pensaste que era el viento
la fuerza de gravedad que te empujaba

Y era el impulso mío
la sed de lo que parte

Bien puede ser
el sol tras la montaña
o la montaña en sombra desteñida
la ciudad que se esfuma en la ventana
la estela en barco convertida
el olor de los muelles

la hora cero
la caída del Dios que nos levanta

La dulzura de las manos solas
la mancha
en los pañuelos blancos

No quise detenerte
me gustabas por agua

Llévate el lobo azul
Déjame el lila pálido

BLUE WOLF

I didn't want to hold you back
you thought it was the wind
the force of gravity pushing you

And it was my impulse
thirst of what goes away

It might as well be
the sun behind the mountain
or the mountain in blemished shade
the city disappearing in the window
the comet transformed into a boat
the odor of the docks

zero hour
God's fall that lifts us

The sweetness of hands alone
the stain
on white handkerchiefs

I didn't want to detain you
I loved you in water

Take the blue wolf
Leave the pale lily for me

RAUL ARIAS
(1943-)

Raul Arias was born in Quito in 1943. He graduated in journalism from the Central University in 1974, where he was active in student politics. It was around that time that Arias joined the Tzántzicos, a group of rebellious young poets and artists, and published his first poems in their magazine, Pucuna. Recently asked if he believed that group had changed the consciousness among writers in Ecuador, he responded: "I think it did, but tempered by what we mean when we speak of changing consciousness, an immense task that really only succeeds in the context of profound, revolutionary, social change. The Tzántzicos influenced culture in Quito and in other cities through their activities at Café 77, their presentations and debates on a variety of artistic subjects, and poetry recitals that almost always drew commentaries of all sorts." Arias has earned awards for his poetry as well as for his theater and radio work.

Among his poetry books: *Poesía en bicicleta* (1975), *Lechuzario* (1983), *Trinofobias* (1988), *Cinemavida* (1995), *Vuelos e inmersiones* (2000), *Caracol en llamas* (2001), and *Pedal de viento* (antología poética, 2004). His 2007 book on the life and poetry of Jorge Carrera Andrade is *La libertad buscando patria*.

LA MÁS BUSCADA

La más buscada,
no tiene precio por inalcanzable;
no usa tacones altos
y anda en desequilibrio todo el tiempo.

De rostro amado
por tajos y cicatrices mal curados;
cuarteada de arriba abajo;
abusada en nuestra casa y en cada casa
donde la nombran miles de bocas extranjeras.

Zigzagueante,
perseguida por balas y misiles,
espiada en mares y en cielos del planeta;
deseada por todos,
menos por los rentistas de la muerte.

Dúctil y dulce fruta,
refrescante y huidiza,
ansiada por los ojos y las manos.

Apenas nació fue violentada,
caricia rota con un manotazo;
inofensiva siempre ofendida,
indolora adolorida,
es la que buscamos:
la paz en cuerpo y alma,
para abrazarla definitivamente
hasta la vida.

THE MOST DESIRED

The most desired,
priceless because unattainable;
she doesn't wear high heels
yet forever walks off balance.

Her beloved face
with its wounds and badly healed scars;
slashed from top to bottom;
abused at our house and every house
where thousands of foreign mouths speak her name.

Zigzagging,
persecuted by bullets and missiles,
spied on across the planet's seas and skies;
desired by all
except by the landlords of death.

Fruit that is ductile and sweet,
refreshing and elusive,
sought by eyes and hands.

No sooner born than raped,
a caress broken by a blow;
harmless but always offended,
painless yet suffering,
we search for her:
peace in body and soul,
to embrace her forever
unto life.

QUE LAS PALABRAS piensen,
se enternezcan, duerman, sueñan y despierten.
Que saliven como gatos ante la leche.
Que oigan alegres el estallido de los cohetes
en una fiesta popular.
Que jueguen como niños en la calle.
Que se saluden en un portal, guareciéndose de la lluvia.
Que las palabras continúen diciendo palabras
y usen pañuelos de colores en el cuello.
Que salgan de sus casas y se conecten
como hilillos de aire o de agua,
pequeños trozos de carne fluyente.
Que, antes que nada, luchen por las otras,
por las encarceladas en la ignorancia
o en las cárceles mismas.
Que las palabras piensen mejor cada día,
que amen la palabra libertad y la defiendan.
Que aprendan a odiar la palabra imposible
y no teman lo desconocido.
Que las palabras peleen, se alisten y desfilen.

IT IS TRUE, words think,
are tender, sleep, dream and wake.
They salivate like cats before milk,
get excited when fireworks go off
at a community fair.
They play like children in the street.
They greet you in a doorway,
sheltering themselves from rain.
Words keep on uttering words
and wear colored handkerchiefs at their necks.
They leave their homes and merge
like delicate threads of water or air,
small flowing chunks of meat.
Before all else, they fight for the others,
those imprisoned by ignorance
or by brick and mortar prisons.
Each day words have deeper thoughts,
they love and defend the word *freedom*.
They learn to hate the word *impossible*
and are not afraid of the unknown.
Words struggle, get ready and fall into line.

SARA VANEGAS
(1950-)

Sara Vanegas was born in Cuenca in 1950. Her family traveled in her childhood but returned to that highland city in 1966. Inspired by a copy of Lorca's *Romancero gitano* that she found in her father's library, Vanegas began writing poetry when she was very young. She published her first poem at the age of 17. She also studied music and was a soprano in the chorus at Casa de la Cultura Ecuatoriana. She studied abroad (in Munich, Germany) and has maintained a connection to that city, where in 1986 she defended her doctoral dissertation, "The Latin American Image in Contemporary German Literature." Vanegas's knowledge of English and German, as well as her love of music, have made her one of her country's most interesting literary critics. She has also published short stories and literature for young readers. She has said of her work: "My poetry is committed, not in the political sense but experimentally."

Among her poetry books are: *90 poemas* (1981), *Luciérnaga y otros textos* (1982), *Entrelíneas* (1987), *Indicios* (1988), *PoeMAR* (1994), *Sara Vanegas Coveña. Poesía junta* (2007), *Mínima antología poética* (2010), and *De la muerte y otros amores* (2014).

TU NOMBRE . . . deja una cicatriz de naves incendiadas
aquí. en el océano de mi pecho

*

el cortejo de lunas es ya un recuerdo en tus ojos náufragos
la noche nos juntará en lo más hondo:
como un aullido

*

el fantasma de tu voz
aún me llama

hoy

por un nombre ya olvidado

*

en ciertas noches del año—dicen—emerge sobre la super-
ficie del océano una ronda de delfines dorados formando
extraños mensajes . . .

la luna entonces se va tornando azulada. lentamente

*

dicen que cuando la luna está azul brotan ciudades enteras
del fondo del mar. que sus habitantes (de ojos fosforescen-
tes y oscuros ropajes) inician entonces una larga danza que
no cesa hasta que algún puerto se arroja a las profundidades

¿quién no ha visto arder el mar en esas noches?

*

mar que me bebes gota a gota
noche a noche

mar que me sorbes
desde tu eternidad amarga

*

voces que reclaman tu garganta. voces oscuras. voces que se
enredan en tu lengua y en tus manos. voces que te atrapan

y te encadenan al mar

*

voces encadenadas

voces que arrastra el mar

de tarde en tarde

*

collar de voces que aprisiona mi garganta

desde su origen tras el agua

YOUR NAME . . . leaves a scar of burning boats
here. in the ocean of my breast

*

the entourage of moons remains a memory in your ship-
wrecked eyes
night will join us in the deepest place:
like a howl

*

the ghost of your voice
continues to call me

today

by a name already forgotten

*

on certain nights of the year—they say—a circle of golden
dolphins rises to the ocean's surface forming strange mes-
sages . . .

then the moon turns blue. slowly

*

they say when the moon is blue whole cities spring from
the bottom of the sea. then their inhabitants (with phos-
phorescent eyes and dark clothing) begin a long dance that
does not end until some port throws itself into the depths

on those nights, who hasn't seen the sea burn?

*

sea that drinks me drop by drop
night after night

sea that sips me
from its bitter forever

*

voices reclaiming your throat. obscure voices. voices that
tangle on your tongue and in your hands. voices that trap you

and chain you to the sea

*

chained voices

voices that drag the sea

from one afternoon to another

*

necklace of voices imprisoning my throat

from its home beyond the water

CATALINA SOJOS
(1951-)

Catalina Sojos was born in Cuenca. At the age of six she recited poems from memory but didn't publish her first book until she was 37. Sojos's poetry has earned her numerous prizes, including the Gabriela Mistral in 1989 and the Jorge Carrera Andrade in 1992. Her work has been translated into English, French, Portuguese and Italian. She also writes prose and literature for children. She is the director of the Manuel A. Landivar site museum and writes for the El Mercurio newspaper in Cuenca.

Among her poetry books are: *Hojas de poesía* (1989), *Fuego* (1990), *Tréboles marcados* (1991), *Fetiches* (1995), *Cantos de piedra y agua* (1999, 20018), *Láminas de la memoria* (1999), *Escrito en abril* (2009), *Antología personal* (2010), and *Ecuador* (2015).

RUINAS (FRAGMENTOS)

I

a la primera palabra le ofrecimos un poncho de espóndilos
y en sus tobillos atamos sonajeras

cuando la noche se volvió hueso
ella huyó con su aire

luego quedamos manchas
de aquellos que creímos danzar en su esqueleto

II

cuentan que el corazón del inca se transformó en aríbalo
sus fragmentos se exhiben
con esa terca actitud de las cosas que sobreviven al olvido

III

jamás sabrás quién es el vigilado

los pasos van y vienen
detrás del muro con las cinco hornacinas

arde la luna en la piedra sacrificial

hay un olor a escombro
a tierra retorcida

no, nunca habrás de saber
quién es el vigilante, el vigilado

IV

nadie entiende qué hace una mujer
como si fuera un pájaro muerto entre el cielo y la tierra

en tanto el vacío se instaura
ella limpia su corazón entre las piedras

V

ellos cuentan su historia con los dedos
y en los nudos inventan poliedros

registran el horizonte con hilos verdes
su tacto dibuja púas en los ojos

VI

entre las piedras los shamanes ululan

en su memoria
la pequeña hoja de una selva
se mantiene agarrada de su cola

presagios pueblan el bosque
lejos de la ceniza que en ti se confabula

VII

qué tiempo de exactitud sepultado entre ortigas

sal de la piedra
hombre que fue maíz y hierba húmeda

bajo rotas columnas
y amargas trenzas

tendido estás
en la delgada lengua del olvido

Ruins (fragments)

I

at the first word we offered her a poncho of stressed syl-
lables
and adorned his ankles with rattles

when night turned to bone
she and her attitude fled

later we were simply images
of those who believed we danced in her skeleton

II

they tell us the Inca's heart retained an afterglow
its fragments are displayed
with that stubborn attitude of that which survives obscurity

III

you will never know who is being watched

footsteps come and go
behind the wall with five niches

the moon burns on sacrificial stone

there is an odor of debris
of devious earth

no, you will never know
who is the watched, who watches

IV

no one knows what a woman does
pretending to be a dead bird suspended between heaven
and earth

while emptiness establishes itself
she scours her heart among the stones

V

they tell her story on their fingers
and invent pyramids in their knuckles

they measure the horizon with green threads
their touch pierces her eyes

VI

shamans sway among the stones

in her memory
the small jungle leaf
is still attached to her tail

omens flood the forest
far from the ash that conspires within you

VII

what precise time buried among nettles

salt of stone
man who was corn and humid herb

beneath broken columns
and bitter braids

you are laid out
upon oblivion's narrow tongue

JENNIE CARRASCO
(1955-)

Jennie Carrasco was born in Ambato. She is a poet and narrator who is also a university professor. Like so many others, she got her literary start in the workshop run by Miguel Donoso Pareja. She has a post-graduate degree in cultural heritage and administration, and sustainable tourism. Carrasco has done many things throughout her life, including working with the press and on women's issues. She has led holistic therapy workshops in creativity, identity and self-esteem with an emphasis on Gestalt and the creative process. In her book *Espíritu jaguar* she works with themes from the Ecuadoran Amazon that describe the life of the Amazonian peoples and their use of magical powers. She has appeared in a number of anthologies and participated in international poetry events in Mexico, El Salvador, Venezuela, France and Ecuador. Her work has earned her a number of prizes in short story, journalism and poetry contests; she has also judged several of those contests.

Among her poetry books, short story collections and novels are: *Antología del cuento feminista latinoamericano* (1987), *De cara al mundo* (1995), *En busca del cuento perdido* (1996) *Toros en el corazón* —co-author— (1997), *Antología de narradoras ecuatorianas* (1997), *Antología básica del cuento ecuatoriano* (1998), *Quiero vivir y nunca le conté a nadie* (1998), *Poesía erótica de mujeres: Antología del Ecuador* (2001), *Arañas en mi vestido de seda, De diosas, guerreras y mujeres, Del infierno al paraíso, Una vuelta más abuela, De noche el negro sueño, Confesiones apocalípticas, La diosa en el espejo, Cuentos de ceniza y Amor distorsionado, Viaje a ninguna parte* (2004 y 2016), *La diosa en el espejo, Cuentos de ceniza y Amor distorsionado,* and *Espíritu jaguar* (2017).

MIEDO

Durante toda mi vida
cargué a mis espaldas
el miedo de los hombres
no era un miedo mío
era el de mi padre
el de mi marido y de mi hermano
el de todos mis amantes
el miedo de mis hijos

Me pesaban esos temores malheridos
guerras, gritos ciegos
el fuego que al principio descubrieron
se volvió devastador
yo, mujer de aguas oscuras
de aire negro
sólo en la luna me reconocía

No era un miedo mío
yo dominaba los secretos de las flores
y los rincones más profundos
sembré y coseché
mi sangre fecunda
dio a luz la vida y la muerte
día tras día, siglo tras siglo
me parí a mí misma

Vagando en la nada pregunto
¿cómo matar el miedo de los hombres?
¿Cómo matar mi propio miedo?

FEAR

All my life
I have carried men's fear
on my back,
not my own fear
but my father's
husband's and brother's
the fears of all my lovers
the fears of my sons

Those damaged fears weighed on me,
wars, blind screams,
at first the fire they revealed
turned devastating
I, a woman of dark waters
and somber air
could see myself only in the moon

It wasn't my fear,
I owned the secrets of flowers
and hidden places,
I planted and harvested,
my fertile blood
gave birth to life and death
day after day, century upon century
I birthed myself

Wandering in nothingness I ask
how can we kill men's fear?
How can I kill my own?

CARACOLES AFRICANOS

El collar de caracoles africanos
que me regalaste
me dejó en el pecho el fuego de tu pueblo
el efluvio de tambores y gacelas

Es brujería, dice mi vecina
vil manejo de tu espíritu
no sabe que atravesé sabanas y marismas
para llegar al límite
y tragar las espumas de tu ámbar

En otras latitudes me habrían lapidado
pero en este pedazo de selva
en este río de café
me beben en secreto, me visten
porque me atreví a lamer tu piel mandinga
porque recibí los deleites de tu cuerpo
y me interné en los meandros de tu esencia

Bruja, repite mi vecina
como eco, chillido, alboroto
los caracoles han hecho lo suyo:
tu cuerpo diletante me respira
tu tallo de jade me fecunda

AFRICAN COWRIE

The necklace of African cowrie
you gave me
left the fire of your people
an outpouring of drums and gazelles in my breast.

My neighbor says it is witchcraft
an evil that manipulates your spirit
she doesn't know I crossed plains and marshlands
to reach the farthest edge
and swallow your amber's foam

In other latitudes they'd have stoned me
but in this bit of forest
along this river of coffee
they drink me in secret, wear me
because I dared lick your Mandingo skin
receive your body's delights and immerse myself
in the meanders of your power

Witch, my neighbor says again
repetitious echo, shriek, incitement,
the cowrie have done their work:
your incipient body breathes me
your jade stalk plants its seed

SARA PALACIOS
(1955-)

Sara Palacio is from Quito, where she combines sculpture, poetry, and the promotion of interdisciplinary cultural events, often at her own gallery where she organizes exhibitions by Ecuadoran and international artists. Palacios studied communication at the Central University and ceramics at CREA. She has shown her own sculpture in individual and group shows in Ecuador and other countries. She got her start in poetry with Ulises Estrella at the Laboratory of the Image and the Word. Xavier Oquendo has written of her poetry that it "obliges the reader to think, to reflect on the terrible simplicity of things." Of artistic expression she herself writes: "Returning to the same point is to retreat; if you move in a circle, just lifting yourself a bit, you trace a spiral."

Her books of haiku and other brief poems, some editions richly illustrated by the author, are: *Pequeñas zoologías humanas* (1998, 1999, 2001, 2006, 2007, 2008) and *Él y Mas pequeñas zoologías humanas.*

LA BALLENA

La ballena sufre para ser amada
se entristece para ser amada
se emborracha para ser amada
baila, mueve las manos para ser amada
hace poemas para ser amada
y por fin . . . es amada.
Entonces
salta, con su enorme cuerpo
se hunde en el agua y se va
sin importarle nada
porque es ballena.

THE WHALE

The whale suffers for love
sorrows for love
gets drunk for love
dances, moves its hands to be loved
writes poems to be loved
and finally . . . is loved.
Then
it leaps, its enormous body
disappears underwater and leaves
without a thought in the world
because it is a whale.

EL ÁGUILA

Haré una lista de todas las cosas que necesito
en caso de catástrofe, piensa el águila circunspecta.
Un temblor interior le hace pensar que ha llegado el ter-
remoto.
Abre los ojos, vuelve a presionar su muslo exuberante
y nuevamente el temblor.
Petrificada mira a su alrededor
para comprobar la inminencia del acto telúrico,
pero . . . nada.

THE EAGLE

I will make a list of everything I need
in case of catastrophe, the eagle is cautious.
An inner shudder warns of approaching earthquake.
It opens its eyes, squeezes its exuberant muscle once more
and there's that shudder again.
Petrified, it looks around
ready for imminent telluric movement,
but there is . . . nothing.

HIENA MIRÓ A TORTUGA

Hiena miró a tortuga
palpitando dentro de su caparazón,
pensó: horrible animal innecesario.
Sin embargo,
adquirió un collar de carey
lo lució ante los demás animales
haciendo hincapié en su amistad
con el pleurodiras reptil.

HYENA LOOKS AT TORTOISE

Hyena looking at tortoise
throbbing within its shell,
mused: horrible irrelevant animal.
Nevertheless,
it got ahold of a tortoiseshell collar
and flaunted it before the other animals
emphasizing its friendship with the pleurodira
who could draw its head back to its heart.

MARITZA CINO ALVEAR
(1957-)

Maritza Cino Alvear was born in Guayaquil where she graduated in Spanish Language and Literature from the Catholic University. Her work has appeared in numerous national and international anthologies and has been translated into English, French and Italian. In 2009, Cino Alvear represented Ecuador at Mexico's Gathering of Poets of the Latino World. She teaches at several universities in Guayaquil and coordinates the creative writing workshops at that city's Center of Art.

Among her poetry collections are: *Algo parecido al juego* (1983), *A cinco minutos de la bruma* (1987), *Invenciones del retorno* (1992), *Entre el juego y la bruma* (anthology, 1995), *Infiel a la sombra* (2000), and *Cuerpos guardados* (2008).

CUERPOS GUARDADOS

1

Infiel a mi sombra original
he atravesado efigies y pirámides,
me he acercada a la prehistoria
del placer
con la clarividencia de lo breve.

La sanación ha llegado,
en tinieblas
cuando menos la esperaba
devastando cábalas y adioses.

2

En este manuscrito reposan las sustancias
de antiguos ritos destinados a los mares,
de esa mitad de eternidad que me persigue
en un memorial ausente de palabras.

Esta ceremonia no es sagrada
solo un oleaje de sintagmas
en el ojal de una blusa desgastada
por el rumor del olvido y la ironía.

La otra mitad de eternidad
desconoce la rutina y el silencio,
voces que se mutan en esencias
de una escritura que conspira en mi retina.

3

Me acosa la etimología del no decir
asignando la escritura a un lugar común
repetirme en el sonido del agua,
cada vocablo me conduce al origen.

Las mismas palabras se anuncian
caricaturas en blanco y negro,
cualquier pista es una huella ausente.

Una nueva parodia me atrapa
la cotidianidad me libera.
Me entrego al sonido del fuego.

4

Dejé de escribir
con la exactitud del calendario
después de que me embalsamaran sus textos
y me convirtiera en pirámide.

Ahora lo sé
por sus olores mortales
signos de luto
que fermentan las tumbas,

mientras yo transito invertida
con otra voz que me viene,
de la escritura de un dios
que no es el dios de los muertos.

5

Perdida en un paraíso
de pertenencias inéditas

buscadora de ciénagas
instalo el deseo.

Lentamente me toca
desde esta página en blanco,
su palidez me entretiene
de este silencio de historias,
me asigna placeres en una nueva versión.
Su movimiento es un río
que no alcanzo a editar.

6

No invento la vida
permanece intacta.
Las mismas cosas discurren
en este clásico momento.

La ciudad narrada con sus recurrentes calles,
el paso de los días ausentes de metáforas,
los nombres confusos y la medida del deseo.

Me deslumbro ante este único momento,
contemplar y convertirme
en un clásico lugar común.

7

Empiezo a olvidar
mi primer alumbramiento,

el placer de nombrar
lo singular de mis genes.

Comienzo a creer
que la ciudad me dispersa

hacia una escena
donde los sentidos se turban.

Compruebo la errancia
de una palabra difusa
que se confunde en el agua
cuando la memoria olvida.

8

Persigo las palabras
simulando las edades del misterio.

Este cuerpo huye
de visiones ancestrales
sin memoria.

9

Que la escritura no me toque
y su tono no me llegue,
que este festín de sonidos
no me interrogue el sueño,
que no me toque la vida
ni el aullido del sol.

Que este elenco de miradas y de lluvias solas
no desemboque en los nombres de Dios.

Que la escritura no me invada
con su magia evanescente
en mi última función.

Hidden Bodies

1

Unfaithful to my first shadow
I have traveled effigies and pyramids,
approached the prehistory
of pleasure
with barely perceptible clairvoyance.

Healing has arrived,
when least expected
in shadows threatening cabalas and farewells.

2

The substances live in this manuscript
of ancient rites headed for the sea,
from this half of eternity that stalks me
with a wordless monument.

This ceremony is not sacred,
only a surge of phrases
from the buzz of irony and oblivion
in the buttonhole of a worn-out blouse.

Eternity's other half
knows nothing of routine and silence,
voices muted in the essence of writing
conspiring in my retina.

3

The etymology of silence stalks me,
assigns writing to cliché,
repeats the sound of water,
every word takes me back to the beginning.

The same words present themselves
as black and white caricatures,
any trail is an invisible footprint.

A new parody claims me,
the commonplace sets me free.
I give myself to the sound of fire.

4

After they embalmed my texts
and turned me into a pyramid,
I stopped writing in accordance
with a precise calendar.

Now I know the signs
of keening
by their mortal odors
fermenting tombs,

while I pass by in reverse
with another voice that comes,
possessed by the writing of a god
not the god of the dead.

5

Lost in a paradise
of unpublished attachments,
searcher of swamps
I take possession of desire.

From this blank page
it caresses me slowly,
its ghostly visage keeps me company,
assigns me new versions of pleasure
in this history of silences.

Its movement is a river
I cannot begin to edit.

6

I do not invent life,
it remains intact.
The same things happen
in this iconic moment.

The city narrated in repeated streets,
a passage of days without metaphor,
confusing names and the measure of desire.

I am blinded by this singular instant,
contemplating and becoming
a classic cliché.

7

I begin to forget
my first birth,

the pleasure of naming
my own genes.

I begin to believe
that the city scatters me
to a place
where my senses are confused.

8

I follow words that pretend
to be ages of mystery.

This body flees
ancestral visions
devoid of memory.

9

Let writing fail to touch me
and its tone not come close,
may this feast of sounds
not interrogate my dreams,
may it not touch my life
nor its howl of sun.

May this cast of glances and lonely rains
not lead to God's names.

May writing not invade me
with its luminous magic
in my final act.

CARMEN VÁSCONES
(1958-)

Carmen Váscones was born in Samborondón, Guayas province. She graduated in psychology and clinical psychology and has engaged in research and consulting as well as working in institutions that attend to children, families and the community. Váscones also gives literary workshops and has taught at colleges and universities. Her work has won numerous awards in biennales and contests.

Among her books are: *La muerte un ensayo de amores* (1991, 1994), *Con/fabulaciones* (1992), *Memorial a un acantilado* (1994), and *Aguaje* (1999).

POEMA

El acuario revuelve la oquedad del pez
La mitad de una concha ilumina al marino
Que no pudo salir del sueño

La sirena fue una presencia inesperada

Entre cristales el cantar de los días
Sucede el carnaval
Viene la cuaresma...

La duda solloza su olvido

El cráter confiesa sobre la ciudad
Su círculo recorre la intimidad de una correspondencia
La vertiente del nudo cambia la rotación
La nevada una centrífuga del ciclo
Los ciclos de la llegada entonaron un eco de hábitos

Las historietas tras los despuntes del topo
La hiena pisa el esquema del degollador

La banda suelta día a día la torsión del tenor
El desbande aplasta algo dejado a la intemperie
Los modos del espectador resuenan en el génesis cancelado

El pasado levanta la efigie infantil

El paso de una reverencia elogia la inocencia
Con una noche oral desprendiéndose en el horizonte

El estilete recorta una hazaña
La sepultura conmemora su advenimiento

El ideal: un soplo de amor de cuerpo a cuerpo

El tribunal absuelve su propia condena
Un azar disecado en cada cuerpo

La colonia de caníbales acecha la historia

La nada: un silencio pegado a la huella
Baila sobre el cadáver del encomendado

El universo parece un ángel decapitado cayendo en el
átomo

El color del círculo marcó la salida
Un deseo centrípeto acompaña la fuga
El destino se fragmenta en persecuciones

El fugitivo cruzó la frontera
Se acerca al reposo
Deja de huir
Se entrega a él.

POEM

The aquarium moves through the fish's cavity
A half shell illuminates the sailor
Unable to emerge from his dream

An unexpected mermaid

Carnival comes around
Lent arrives
Days sing among crystals . . .

Doubt sobs its oblivion

The crater pleads guilty above the city
Circumference travels relationship's intimacy
The knot's gradient changes direction
Snow is a centrifuge in the cycle
Patterns of arrival leave an echo of customs

Comic books follow the mole's dawn
The hyena steps on the executioner's blueprint

Day after day the band turns loose the tenor's torque
A mad rush tramples something left outdoors
The spectator's manners sound in cancelled genesis

The past raises a childlike effigy

A passing reverence applauds innocence
With a vocal night taking leave of the horizon

The stiletto slashes a deed
Burial commemorates its accession

The ideal: a breath of love from one body to another

The tribunal absolves the sentence it hands down
Desiccated luck in every body

A colony of cannibals stalks history

Nothing: silence stuck to a footprint
Dancing on the corpse of the trusted one

The universe is like a decapitated angel falling inside an
atom

Circle's color signals the exit
A centripetal desire accompanies escape
Destiny fragments into abuse

A fugitive crossed the border
Sleep draws near
Stop fleeing
It gives itself to him.

RAÚL VALLEJO
(1959-)

Raúl Vallejo was born in Manta. He is a novelist, poet, essayist and university professor. He was educated at the Colegio Salesiano Cristóbal Colón and the Universidad Católica de Santiago de Guayaquil, graduating in Spanish Language and Literature in 1984. Vallejo also attended the University of Maryland, College Park, as a Fulbright Scholar, where he earned his Master of Arts degree in Literature. He received his Ph.D. at the Universidad Pablo de Olavide, Seville, in 2014. In 1976, Vallejo was part of the editorial board of *Sicoseo* magazine. From 1982 to 1985 he attended Miguel Donoso Pareja's writers' workshop, another poet nurtured in that venue. Vallejo has served as Minister of Education on a number of occasions, as Ecuador's Ambassador in Colombia, and more recently as Minister of Culture. In 2007 the Ecuadorian Government recognized his public service with the Orden Nacional al Mérito, Gran Cruz. He currently heads the Literature department at the University of the Arts in Guayaquil.

To date, his poetry collections are: *Cánticos para Oriana* (2003), *Crónica del mestizo* (2007), *Missa solemnis* (2008), and *Mística del tabernario* (2015).

POETA INDIGNADO:

El 10 de mayo de 1975, el Ejército Revolucionario del Pueblo
ajustició a un poeta de la insurrección popular de El Salvador.

    Dalton García, Roque Antonio
    de las tierras del pulgarcito de América: 1,70 de estatura—
    tez blanca ojos castaño oscuros—nariz grande—boca
pequeña—
    cabello negro
    excesivamente poeta para ser militante
    y sin embargo militante hasta la muerte.

Tus propios compañeros
  te capturaron
    te juzgaron
      te ejecutaron
te ejecutamos con el repudio académica a tu poesía
muy ideológica, panfletaria, política como tu vida
    —guanaco hijo de la gran puta—

Pobrecito poeta que era él, en qué taberna de qué otros lugares
su muerte sin sentido nos dejó una herida honda
infectada de sectarismo, la política,
agotamiento de la palabra por exceso de uso
aunque te pese y nos pese: tú eres un gran muerto
y los que continuamos vivos y en paz, tus grandes asesinos.

La poesía fue fusilada junto con la fragilidad de tu cuerpo.

Y, ENTONCES

POETA INDIGNADO:

Y, entonces,
¿para qué escribo?
¿para quién escribo?

La literatura debe ser un bálsamo para el estrés, no este sinsentido
que me tomará por asalto y desnudará el oxímoron en el que existo.

¿Qué valor tiene mi palabra si yo mismo soy un pozo de miedos,
polvareda que se levanta para convertirme en imagen difuminada
del ser que soy, proliferación de identidades, penitente del verso,
perenne forma en movimiento hacia nueva forma contradictoria?

Como los escritores ya no somos vanguardia de nada,
[¿es que alguna vez lo fuimos?] la política nos apesta   ahora
los escritores somos mercancía exhibida en el mercado de las
vanidades.

INDIGNANT POET:

On May 10th, 1975, the People's Revolutionary Army murdered
a poet of El Salvador's popular insurrection.

>   Dalton García, Roque Antonio
>   of the Tom Thumb-sized American nation: height 5 foot 9—
>   white skin, dark brown eyes—large nose—small mouth—
>   black hair
>   too much of a poet to be an activist
>   yet an activist to his death.

Your own comrades
  imprisoned you
    judged you
      executed you
we executed you with our academic rejection of your poetry
too ideological, propagandistic, as political as your life
      —*Salvadoran son of a bitch*—

Poor little poet that he was, in what taverns of other cities
did his senseless death leave its deep wound
infected by sectarianism, politics,
exhaustion of the word by overuse
although it weighs on you and on us: you are a great death
and those of us still alive and living in peace, your great assassins.

In your fragile body poetry met the firing squad.

WHY DO I WRITE?

INDIGNANT POET:

Why do I write?
For whom do I write?

Literature should be a balm for stress, not this meaningless script
that will take me by surprise, undressing the oxymoron in which
I exist.

What value has my word if I myself am a well of fears,
dust rising to turn me into a blurred image
of myself, proliferation of identities, penitent of verse,
perennial voice reaching for a new and contradictory voice?

As we writers are no longer any sort of vanguard,
[were we ever?] politics stink   now
we are merely merchandize displayed in the market of vanities.

EDWIN MADRID
(1961-)

Edwin Madrid is from Quito. He is a poet, editor and essayist. Currently he heads the Writing Workshop at the Casa de la Cultura Ecuatoriana and is the director of the Ediciones de la Línea Imaginaria publishing house. In 2011 he enjoyed a literary residency in Saint-Nazaire, France. Madrid's work has received numerous awards, including the prestigious Casa de las Américas poetry prize in 2004, his country's 2013 Ministry of Culture and Patrimony prize, and the Ecuadorian Writers of the Nineties prize. Madrid's poems have appeared in many anthologies and magazines.

Among his poetry collections are: ¡OH! *Muerte de pequeños senos de oro* (1987), *Enamorado de un fantasma* (1990*)*, *Celebriedad* (1992), *Caballos e iguanas* (1993), *Tentación del otro* (1995), *Tambor sagrado y otros poemas* (1995), *Open Doors* (2000), *Puertas abiertas* (2001), *Mordiendo el frío* (2004), *Lactitud cero°* (2005),*La búsqueda incesante* (2006), *Mordiendo el frío y otros poemas* (2009, 2010), *Pavo muerto para el amor* (2012), *Pararrayos* (2012), *Al Sur del Ecuador* (2014), *Todos los Madrid, el otro Madrid* (2016), and *Au Sud de l´ équateur* (2016) *Mordendo o frio, livro completo* (2016).

LAS ENCANTADAS

Son erupciones volcánicas aparecidas en el mar.
Superficies rugosas, calcáreas y negras, cicatrices del tiempo.
Al principio no existía vida, entonces llegaron las aves y
depositaron semillas incluidas en su excremento o en el fango
adherido a sus patas, otras pepitas resistentes al agua llegaron
por el mar desde el continente suramericano, troncos flotantes
que transportan iguanas, tortugas que emergieron del mar
y se convirtieron en gigantes terrestres, animales habituándose
al alimento hallado en las islas. La ley del más fuerte.
Fue la selección natural.
Galápagos está a mil kilómetros de mí, pero a los dos
nos atraviesa la línea equinoccial. He escuchado relatos
de bucaneros y filibusteros atracando en ellas,
mas no conozco Galápagos.
Sito de naturalistas, alemanes locos, que se refugiaron
y pelearon contra la naturaleza y contra sus almas.

No conozco pero imagino si Gauguin, en vez de Tahití,
llegaba a Galápagos: la vida reptil y el siseo retratados
con retorcida, doblada y petrificada lava negra
dando lugar a saurios antediluvianos y prisioneros
calcinados en medio de una rala y esquelética maleza
como si hubiesen sido quemados por un rayo.
Todo bajo un cielo bochornoso y encapotado en el que
despuntan conos volcánicos, entre los que se deslizan
tortugas gigantes resoplando, o iguanas cruzándose
torpemente como diablillos de las tinieblas.
Pinturas dignas de todos los diablos pero no de Gauguin.
Darwin se sintió atrapado por esos retratos de las Galápagos
Y se adentró en el misterio de los misterios.
No conozco Galápagos, he leído la prosa amenazante
de Melville con grandes cactos, lastre negro poblado

de monstruos y aves color tierra posando sobre su cabeza; para él los marinos malvados eran convertidos en tortugas, un archipiélago maldito salido después del final del mundo.

No conozco Galápagos y soy suelo calcinado, lengua partida y escarceada por el sol, la sal corroyendo huesos, roca áspera que repta y atrapa los colores quietos del monótono horizonte azul, descubrimiento, escondite, agua chocando contra la creación divina, vida rota, detenida a ristre para adaptarse a los tiempos. No conozco Galápagos, lenta tortuga contra los rayos del cielo y las corrientes del mar. Soy roca áspera que repta el suelo calcinado, corroído descubrimiento de los colores quietos, creación divina chocando contra la vida, horizonte azul monótono de huesos en las corrientes adaptándose al sol, escondite detenido al cielo y a sus rayos calcinados. No conozco Galápagos, soy vida del cielo y del mar, creación del tiempo, colores ásperos, agua que corroe a los tiempos, divina roca, lengua de hueso escarceada, descubrimiento de las corrientes que reptan en horizonte, suelo en ristre calcinado, a los dos nos atraviesa la línea equinoccial.

THE BEWITCHED

Volcanic eruptions rising out of the sea.
Broken black limestone surfaces, scars of time.
In the beginning there was no life, then birds came
and deposited the seeds in their excrement or in
the mud they carried on their feet, other water-resistant seeds
came by sea from South America, floating branches
bringing iguanas, tortoises that rose from the waves
and became terrestrial giants, animals accustoming
themselves to the food they found on the islands.
It was the law of the strongest. Natural selection.
The Galápagos are a thousand miles from me
but the equator runs through us both. I have heard
stories of attacks by buccaneers and pirates
but I have never been to the Galápagos.
A place of naturalists, crazy Germans who took refuge
there, fighting nature and their own souls.

I don't know but imagine if instead of Tahiti Gauguin
had gone to the Galápagos: reptile life and its hissing sounds
traced in black, twisted, folded and petrified lava
making way for antediluvian sauria and prisoners
calcified in sparse skeletal underbrush
as if they'd been struck by a bolt of lightning.
All beneath a muggy overcast sky
where volcanic cones appear, among which giant tortoises
huff and puff, iguanas move clumsily like little devils in
the shadows. Painting worthy of all devils by Gauguin.
Darwin was drawn by these stories of the Galápagos
and entered that mystery of mysteries.
I don't know the Galápagos, I have read Melville's
threatening prose with its great cacti, black wasteland
inhabited by monsters and earth-colored birds

settling on his head; for him malevolent mariners
were turned into turtles, an evil archipelago
that emerged after the world ended.

I do not know the Galápagos and I am burnt earth, a tongue
split and trodden by the sun, sun corroding bones, sharp rock
that creeps and traps calm color of the horizon's monoto-
nous blue, discovery, hiding place, water crashing against
divine creation, broken life, stopped and ready to adapt
to the times. I do not know the Galápagos, slow tortoise
against sky's rays and currents of the sea. I am sharp rock
creeping across burnt earth, corroded discovery of quiet col-
ors, divine creation battling life, monotonous blue horizon of
bones on the currents adapting themselves to the sun, hiding
place belonging to the sky and its burnt rays. I do not know
the Galápagos, I am the life of sky and sea, time's creation,
sharp colors, water corroding time, divine rock, tongue of
trodden bone, discovery of the currents that creep across the
horizon, burnt earth at the ready, and both of us pierced by
the equator.

NOCHES DE GRANADA

Estoy en Granada
El sol pica la piel y
tu recuerdo pica mi corazón.
¿No sé que hago junto al Lago de Nicaragua?
Es un mar que topa los volcanes
y yo me hundo en las aguas negrísimas de tus ojos.
Voy de isleta en isleta
mirando como viven los nicaragüenses
¿Qué hago en Nicaragua,
38 grados a la sombra,
si mi nostalgia por ti
alcanza los 40 grados en la noche?
Granada,
ciudad de casas azules y verdes y amarillas
e imagino que en aquel patio de paredes rojas
tú bailas y me esperas
mas yo solo
recorro las calles
en busca de una lata de cerveza.
¿Qué hago aquí?
Gioconda Belli lee sus poemas
y Cardenal
y otros cientos de poetas
pero ningún poema dice
cuánto te extraño estas noches.

GRANADA NIGHTS

I'm in Granada
The sun burns my skin and
you burn in my heart.
What am I doing on Lake Nicaragua?
It is a sea with a backdrop of volcanoes
and I submerge myself in the dark liquid of your eyes.
I go from one tiny island to another
observing how Nicaraguans live
What am I doing in Nicaragua,
100 degrees in the shade,
if my longing for you
reaches 104 at night?
Granada,
city of blue and green and yellow houses
and I imagine you in that patio of red walls
dancing and waiting for me
yet I
roam these streets
looking for a bottle of bear.
What am I doing here?
Gioconda Belli reads her poems
and Cardenal
and hundreds of other poets
but none of their poems tell
how I miss you on these nights.

ARIRUMA KOWII
(1961-)

Ariruma Kowii (Tree of Peace) was formerly known as Jacinto Conejo Maldonado. He was born in Otavalo and is a writer, poet and indigenous leader of the Kichwa (Quechua) nation. He is considered one of the most important poets writing in his native language. Kowi graduated in Social and Political Sciences at Ecuador's Central University. He writes for Quito's daily newspaper, "Hoy." He has worked with the National Confederation of Indigenous Peoples of Ecuador and studied the use of therapeutic plants as well as Kichwa culture and literature. In 2007 Kowi was named undersecretary of Education for Indigenous Peoples in the country's Ministry of Education and given responsibility for intercultural dialogue. Currently he heads the School of Letters at the Simón Bolívar University of the Andes and coordinates a professorship of Latin American Indigenous Peoples at the same institution.

Among his books are: *Mutsuktsurini* (1988), *Tsaitsik: poemas para construir el futuro* (1993), and *Diccionario de nombres quechuas* (1998).

SHIMIKUNAKA

Shimikunaka, kawsaytami charin
Wiñachinata, wañuchinata
Ushanllami
Shimikunaka tupu, huyaypash, kayta
ushanllami
Shimika achka kamaktami charin
Huyani nikpika
Mana riksishka pachakunata
riksichinllami
mitimay kawsaytapash
karanllami
shimika, inti, killami kan
shimika, kawsaypa llantumi
kan.

*

Las palabras tienen vida
tienen la capacidad de construirnos
o destruirnos
La palabra tiene tanto poder
que, por ejemplo, un "te quiero"
puede catapultarnos
a dimensiones inexploradas
o exiliarnos en el vacío.
La palabra es el sol, es la luna
es la huella
de nuestro existir.

*

Words are alive
they can create
or destroy us
A word has such power
that, for instance, "I love you"
can launch us
into unknown dimensions
or exile us to the void.
A word is the sun, the moon,
the footprint
of our existence.

MAKIPURARINA

Ñawpamanta kawsaykunaka makimpurarinmi:
Samaywan rikurin, rimankuna,
Shimikunaka, samashka, achikyashka,
huanushka pachamanta shimikunami kan
shinallatak, yuyaykunaka
tamiamanta, intipachamanta wayumi kan
kay pachakunata wayllayachin
shamuk pachakunata
kawsana munaywan, watachin.

•

El pasado y el presente se dan la mano:
se miran serenos, dialogan.
Cada palabra es fruto
de tiempos reposados, iluminados, abonados.
Cada expresión es el fruto
de inviernos y veranos equilibrados
que hacen reverdecer el presente
que auguran un futuro asediado
por el deseo incansable de la vida.

•

The past and present hold hands:
look serenely at one another, converse.
Each word is the fruit
of tranquil illuminated fertile times.

Each expression the product
of winters and summer in equilibrium
causing the present to bloom
predicting a future besieged
by the insatiable desire for life.

XAVIER OQUENDO
(1972-)

Xavier Oquendo was born in Ambato. He has worked as a professor of literature and as a journalist. He is an important promoter of poetry, for the past 14 years organizing and directing the Festival de Poesía Paralelo Cero, a yearly gathering of international as well as local poets who travel the country reading their work in a dozen cities. Oquendo also directs ElAngel, a publishing house with more than one hundred poetry titles to its credit. The extensive anthology of Ecuadorian poetry he published with La Cabra in Mexico (2011) still stands as a major reference. Some of his poetry has been translated into Italian, French, English, Portuguese and Arabic.

Among his poetry collections are: *Guionizando poematográficamente* (1993), *Detrás de la vereda de los autos* (1994), *Calendariamente poesía* (1995), *El (An)verso de las esquinas* (1996), *Después de la caza* (1998), *La Conquista del Agua* (2001), *Salvados del naufragio (1990-2005)*, *Esto fuimos en la felicidad* (2009), *Alforja de caza* (2012), and *El cántaro con sed* (2017). He is also responsible for the following anthologies: *Ciudad en verso (Antología de nuevos poetas ecuatorianos* 2002) and *Antología de nuevos poetas ecuatorianos* (2002).

MI ABUELO Y MI ABUELA

tenían un caminar maduro.
Ella, pausada en el galope;
él, acelerado y discurrido.

Caminaban, mirando la última huella
que había dejado el animal de turno.
Ella seguía el paso del hombre
como una secuencia natural.

El río de mi abuelo
y de mi abuela
no se parece al Guadalquivir
ni al Guayas.
Es un río de piedra que desciende
sobre las sendas
que faltan por conocer
y adentrarse.

Mi abuela nada tiene que ver
con la abuela de Perencejo.
Perencejo no tiene esos senderos
ni ese paso seguro y lento.
El abuelo de Fulano
no conoce el camino que mi abuelo guarda
en el bolsillo:
sendero extraviado
entre la menta y el «king» sin filtro
que olían sus pantalones.

Mi abuelo se parece a los astros.
Mi abuela es un astro.

Mi abuelo se parece a mi abuela
y los dos a las estrellas.

Nada tienen del Guayas ni del Guadalquivir.
Ni de los viejos Fulano y Perencejo.
Los miramos
a través de las radiografías de sus huellas.
Miramos sus sendas como esfinges
que heredamos para practicar la fe.
Nada tienen que ver con mis zapatos torcidos.

Caminaron, los dos, el valle hasta la muerte.
Son un río que esconde a las aguas
debajo de las piedras.

MY GRANDFATHER AND GRANDMOTHER

had a mature way of walking.
She hesitant in her purpose;
he in a hurry and flying.

They walked, observant of the footprint
left by the animal that preceded them.
She followed in the steps of her man
as if in natural sequence.

My grandfather's river
wasn't anything like
the Guadalquivir
or Guayas.
It is a river of stone that descends
over trails
yet to be discovered
and explored.

My grandmother wasn't like
So-and-So's grandmother.
So-and-So's grandmother doesn't possess those trails
nor that slow and sure step.
So-and-So's grandfather
doesn't know the pathway my grandfather keeps
in his pocket:
a pathway misplaced
between a mint and the King without filter
that gave his trousers their odor.

My grandfather looks like the stars.
My grandmother is a star.

My grandfather looks like my grandmother
and they both look like stars.

They have nothing to do with the Guayas or Guadalquivir.
Nor with any old So-and-So.
We glimpse them
in the x-rays of their footprints.
We look at their pathways like the sphynxes
we inherit to practice our faith.
They have nothing to do with my crooked shoes.

The two of them walked the valley to death.
They are a river that hides its waters
beneath the stones.

ANTI-ORACIÓN PARA UN DIOS FELIZ

Oyeme tú, señor dios de las fiestas,
gendarme con cara feliz todos los días.
Dios que te tomas el trago de los ángeles.
dios que creaste la llanura alegre de Disneylandia.

Escúchame, tú, dios de la niñez
con sonrisa siempre dispuesta,
con la mejor diadema de la reina
con el más bello zapato de la corte.

Dios que sin ser rico eras de hacienda.
Señor que sabes ganar, en lid buena, la baraja,
Tú, debes escucharme, señor dios de las vecinas bellas
y de sus regalías invisibles.
Rey o reina. Hombre y mujer de los dones culinarios.
Párame oído, señor dios de los asados
en donde saltaron las más líquidas botellas de vino
que nos hizo ver en líquido a las estrellas,
donde cayó el ojo justo en la mina de oro y el petróleo.

Dios mío, que eres un ejército de dulces,
dios del chocolate y los pasteles,
señor del manjar de leche y los biscochos.
Dios que hiciste el ron, el whisky ahumado, la borrachera,
dios que estuviste conmigo y con solo unos pocos niños
en la escuela, haciéndonos cosquillas y felices.
Protector de los pequeños señores populares, de los guapetones
con cara de tabaco de James Dean.
Señor que me hiciste de la mejor talla en pantalones.
Dios que estuviste en el calor y en el frío y en el baile adolescente
justo cuando el corazón estaba templado.

Escúchame, deidad de la felicidad doméstica
dios de las flores y los edificios con vistas al valle o al océano.
Mírame a los ojos, señor de los pulpos con brazos ambidiestros
señor de los misterios más precisos y poblados,
persona que me has mimado tanto:
con la ciencia, con el conocimiento, con las mandarinas.
Que me has dado amaneceres aun bailando,
que me hiciste fuerte cuando debía caer en picada,
que me hiciste conocer el mundo justo
cuando pasó el metro bajo el conducto de aire
del vestido de Marilyn Monroe.

Señor de la alta alcurnia de los felices,
de la alta costura de Chanel y del sastre imitador de elegancia.
Príncipe que me hiciste adolescente en la dicha,
dios de las cosas que brillan estando lejos
y que siguen brillando en cercanía.

Señor de los momentos, de los instantes felices
me diste los cuadernos para garabatear mis sueños buenos
y gente buena de manzana y novias fieles con azúcar
y grandes salones de baile donde dejó el zapato Cenicienta.

Dios de los gatos
que miran por tu nombre sus propios ojos
y luego son tan hundidos en belleza
y tan seres como tú y como tu alfombra
de plumas de querubín y papagayo
Dios que me invitaste a ser humano por tu mundo creador
y feliz y completo: de dos patas y sin arrugas y sin barba rala,
que nunca me lanzaste desde un muro
y que puedo contar la matemática de mis costillas,
no fui ni hípster, nunca me rompí más que de risa,
nunca me drogue más que con viento,
y con las olas de las cordilleras y sus cigarros
que me dabas tú mismo en la sequía.

Escúchame señor de las entregas:
tú que me diste todo el equipaje
para que viaje, para que mire el amor desde el costado
para que se me haga fácil lo difícil,
para ahuyentar a toda sombra del pecado.

Oyeme bien, Dios que hueles a perfumes
señor que no tienes de tortuga,
Dios que pareces una liebre, Debes escucharme,
debes decirme, por qué ahora, por qué, señor, ahora,
en que me has dado todo de todo y para todo
me siento tan en hueco
tan tristemente profundísimo, como el hoyo de guitarra,
tan solito, tan colchón de cabaña de inverno,
tan huérfano de ti y de todos. Tan de llanto.

¿Por qué señor, Dios de la caverna platónica,
estoy llorando justo, aquí, frente a tu fuente?

ANTI-PRAYER FOR A HAPPY GOD

Hear me, lord god of fiestas,
cop who shows a happy face every day.
God who drinks with the angels.
God who created that joyous field called Disneyland.

You, listen up, god of my childhood
with your ever-ready smile,
beauty queen's finest tiara,
prettiest shoe in the court.

God who's not rich but lives on an estate.
Lord who knows how to win at cards,
you must hear me out, lord god of beautiful neighbor girls
and their invisible privilege.
King or queen. Man and woman of culinary skill.
Listen up, lord god of bar-b-ques
where liquid bottles of wine exploded
bringing the stars into watery focus,
where your eyes settled right on the gold mine and oil well.

My god who is a candy army,
god of chocolates and sweets,
lord of cream ambrosia and cookies.
God who made rum, smoked whiskey, the drunken binge,
god who accompanied me and only a few other kids
at school, tickling and making us happy.
Protector of those popular little men, of the handsome ones
with James Dean's cigarette face.
Lord who gave me trousers that fit.
God who was there in the heat and cold of that adolescent dance
just when my heart began to hesitate.

Hear me, deity of domestic bliss
god of flowers and buildings with valley or ocean views.
Look into my eyes, lord of the octopus with ambidextrous arms,
lord of the most precise and populated mysteries,
he who spoiled me so:
with science, with knowledge, with mandarins.
Who brought dawn while I was still dancing,
who made me strong when I should have fallen flat on my face,
who pointed me toward justice
when the metro ran beneath the air duct
lifting Marilyn Monroe's dress.

Lord of the happy ones' noble ancestry,
of Chanel's high fashion and the tailor who mimics elegance.
Prince who turned me adolescent in joy,
god of everything that glitters in the distance
and keeps on glittering close up.

Lord of moments, instants of happiness,
you gave me notebooks to scribble my good dreams
and good apple people, girlfriends faithful to sugar
and great dance halls where Sleeping Beauty left her slipper.

God of cats
who see your name in their own eyes,
and are then so beautiful,
as human as you and your hair piece
of cherubim and parrot feathers.
God who in your creation invited me to be human
and happy and complete: standing on my own two feet
without wrinkles or a mangy beard,
you who never threw me off a wall,
I can count the mathematics of my ribs,
I wasn't a hipster, I never broke but in laughter,
never drugged myself except with the wind

and the waves of the Andes and their cigarettes
that you yourself gave me in the dry times.

Hear me, lord of deliverance:
you who gave me everything I need
for the journey, so I can look at love
out of the corner of my eye,
make easy what is difficult,
bring all the shadows of sin together.

Listen well, perfumed god,
lord unlike a tortoise
and like a hare, you've got to listen to me,
tell me, why now, why now lord,
when you've given me all this and for all time
do I feel like I'm in a pit
so desperately deep, like the chamber of a guitar.
As alone as a cabin mattress in winter,
so orphaned by you and by everyone. So sobbing.

Why, lord, god of Plato's cave, am I crying
here, right here, before your fountain?

JULIA ERAZO
(1972-)

Julia Erazo was born in Quito. She works as a journalist but also teaches language and communication courses and participates in cultural projects throughout the Quito area with the Ministry of Culture and with Casa de la Cultura Ecuatoriana's film program. From 1997 to 2001, she headed Galería Imágenes' cultural center and was editorial assistant at Editorial El Angel until 2013. She is also known as an astute literary critic. She co-edited *La voz habitada: Siete poetas ecuatorianos frente a un nuevo siglo* (2008). Her work has been translated into French, Italian, Portuguese, Arabic and English. She has participated in poetry festivals in Ecuador, Spain, Colombia, Venezuela, Mexico, Cuba, Peru, Argentina and Nicaragua.

Among her books are: *Imágenes de viento y de agua* (2008), *Verbal* (2008), *Tu verano en mis alas & verbal* (2012), and *Euler Granda, Atajos de otra piel* (2013).

TIEMPO MUERTO

A Juan Gelman

Si me dieran a elegir, yo elegiría
esta salud de saber que estamos muy enfermos,
esta dicha de andar tan infelices.
Juan Gelman

—me preocupan los osos polares—
dijo
—se adaptarán, les saldrán escamas bucearán felices en
aguas tibias— respondí

—no debería ser ni malo ni bueno—

nada más y nada menos pensar así
en las especies animales aferrándose a una vida condenada
a la herida y en el homo perversus
mamífero indiferente
creciéndole plumas y cresta para sobrevivir
y sobrevivirse

—habrá que creer— dije de nuevo

dudando de la bondad de mis palabras

inhalando el humo del cigarrillo mutuo
olvidando la existencia de los niños y de la abuela riendo de
la muerte inminente
de los cambios del clima
de nuestro propio cáncer

DEAD TIME

To Juan Gelman

If they let me choose, I would choose
this health of knowing we are very ill,
this joy of living so unhappily.
                    Juan Gelman

—I'm worried about the polar bears—
he said
—they'll adapt, they'll grow scales and fish in warm
waters— I answered

—we mustn't think of it as good or bad—

neither more nor less than such thoughts
about the animal species holding to a life condemned to
the wound and about perverse homo sapiens
indifferent mammals
growing feathers and a comb to survive
and survive us

—we've got to believe— I insisted

doubting the kindness of my words

inhaling the smoke of a shared cigarette
forgetting the existence of children and grandmother
laughing at imminent death
at climate change
at our own cancer

CICATRICES

¿Quién dijo que la herida estaba herida
ahora que la tierra se secó?
Carlos Otero

hay algo en ella que sonríe al subir los escalones de la casa
algo que despierta la danza entre los guacamayos
algo en su mirada donde chocan las olas y saltan los peces
algo que se mueve delicado entre sus piernas

hay algo que hace salir a los sapos de entre la maleza algo
que ha dejado huellas allende sus sandalias
algo en el batir vaporoso de su falda
algo en el viento

que cruza por su cabellera

algo desfigura el paisaje

algo asusta de pronto a los sapos que se esconden algo
empuja a las aves a volar
algo desborda el brillo del océano en sus ojos

algo me inquieta
si voy detrás

algo en sus hombros
algo justo encima del cinto de su falda
algo que su blusa revela tenue en su espinazo

hay algo en esa mujer que no se justifica

SCARS

Who said that the wound was wounded
now that the earth is dry?
                    Carlos Otero

something in her smiles as she climbs the steps to the house
something that causes her to dance among the guacamayos
something in her expression where waves break and fish jump
something trembling between her legs

there is something that lets frogs escape into the brush
something left by the soles of her sandals
something in the vaporous movement of her skirt
something in the wind
                    flowing through her hair

something disfigures the landscape

something suddenly frightens the sheltering frogs
something lifts the birds in flight
something overflows the ocean's brilliance in her eyes

something bothers me
                    when I follow her

something in her shoulders
something just above the waistband of her skirt
something her blouse reveals tenuous along her spine

there is something in that woman that's just not right

RESPUESTA ACUOSA

a Sandra Beraha

si las lágrimas no fueran parte del océano y las palabras no
    fueran los peces
y las esperas unas olas poco benevolentes y las penas el
    alimento que nos
desnuda el frío
y si tú no fueras el mástil y si los otros no nos alzáramos
    como las velas
si el planeta no fuera una brújula o un globo flotante en
    el vacío del universo
si la vida no fuera la ficción de otros pensamientos
si ya no durmiéramos sobre hojas transparentes y si
    despertáramos
al abrazo de nuevos líquidos y antiguas voces
si ya pasáramos la línea del verso y si no quisiéramos más
    que el simple
estado de la arena
mojados y secos
secas y mojadas
removidos y lanzadas
hundidos y montículas

WATERY RESPONSE

to Sandra Beraha

if tears didn't belong to the ocean and words weren't fish
if waiting wasn't tight-fisted waves and sorrow what keeps
    us from cold
and if you weren't the mast and the others didn't overwhelm
    us like sails
if the planet wasn't a compass or globe floating in the
    emptiness of space
if life wasn't the fiction of others' thoughts
if we no longer slept on transparent leaves and woke to
    the embrace
of new liquids and ancient voices
if we'd already gone beyond the poem's line and wanted
    nothing more
than the simplicity of sand
wet and dry
dry and wet
churned and launched
immersed and raised

ANA CECILIA BLUM
(1972-)

Ana Cecilia Blum was born in Guayaquil but cur-
rently lives in Tucson, Arizona. Her early education was in
a catholic convent. She continued her studies in Guayaquil,
at the Vicente Rocafuerte University where she earned a
degree in Political and Social Sciences. During those years,
she also participated in Miguel Donoso Pareja's literary
workshop, and took classes in literary theory at the Catholic
University. Blum taught Language and Communication at
FLACSO and wrote for several literary supplements. For
her work promoting literature, she was named a member
of the Casa de la Cultura Ecuatoriana and the Association
of Contemporary Writers in Chimborazo. In 1999, she
moved to Quito, where she studied the authors of the Latin
American boom at the Universidad Andina Simón Bolívar.
In 2000 she emigrated to the United States, where she did
a post grad in the Spanish Language at Colorado State
University. One of her interests is researching contemporary
Ecuadorian poetry by women.

Among her books are: *Descanso sobre mi sombra* (1995),
Donde duerme el sueño (2005), *La que se fue* (2008), *La voz
habitada* (co-author 2008), *Todos los éxodos* (2012), *Libre de
Espanto* (2012), *Poetas de la Mitad del Mundo, Antología de
Poesía escrita por Mujeres Ecuatorianas* (co-anthologist, 2013),
Absurdities (2014), *Áncoras* (2015), and *Rituales* (2016).

POETICUS

Escribo, porque no puedo pelear batallas con mis manos
y el lápiz—a veces—apunta mejor que la escopeta.

Escribo, porque el verbo escribir suena a única certeza,
y es ruta sin distancias, y es cuerpo sin virus.

Escribo, porque la hoja en blanco es un gato feral
y debo recogerlo, alimentarlo, darle guarida, amarlo.

Escribo, porque los adjetivos acechan y cuando matan,
también dan vida; porque el lugar común no me asusta
y lo que se ha dicho mil veces, igual salpica su encanto.

Escribo, porque todo en mí es un desencuentro:
los terminales se mudan, las calles cambian de nombre,
y nunca atino estaciones, horarios o trabajos, retornos o
partidas.

Escribo porque aunque duele, no duele tanto.

Escribo, para llenar los cántaros,
limpiar los espejos,
empuñar los espacios,
caminar los laberintos.

Escribo, para no morirme de pena.
Por eso escribo . . .

POETICA

I write because I cannot go into battle with my hands
and the pencil—at times—has better aim than the gun.

I write because the verb to write sounds like the only sure thing,
and it's a journey without distances, a body without a virus.

I write because the blank page is a feral cat
I must take in, feed, shelter and love.

I write because adjectives stalk me and when they kill
they also give life; because clichés do not frighten me
and what has been said a thousand times can also delight.

I write because everything in me is missed opportunity:
terminals switch places, streets change their names
and I never get the right station, schedule, job or comings and
goings.

I write because although it hurts it doesn't hurt that much.

I write to fill the jar,
clean my glasses,
push spaces forward,
walk through labyrinths.

I write so I won't die of shame.
That's why I write . . .

DEL RETORNO

Hay calles que te llaman, vidas que te llaman,
metáforas que quieren coagular tu nombre,
una casa en ruinas, pero tu casa.

Ya es hora de cuidar de tus muertos
alimentarlos, vestirlos, sentarlos a la mesa;
ordenar los versos, desempolvar la biblioteca;
devolverte a la quietud de la palabra.

No temas, que el retorno
jamás te quitará los elefantes,
la ballena, el oso pardo,
la montaña, el tornado, los saguaros.
Ellos, serán siempre en la memoria.

OF THE RETURN

There are streets that call to you, lives that call,
metaphors that want to freeze your name,
a house in ruins, but your house.

Now is the hour you must care for your dead
feed them, dress them, seat them at the table;
organize your poems, dust the library;
return yourself to the silence of the word.

Do not fear, the return
will never steal the elephants,
whale, brown bear,
mountain, tornado, saguaros.
They will remain in your memory.

ALEYDA QUEVEDO
(1972-)

Aleyda Quevedo was born in Quito. She is a poet, journalist, literary essayist and cultural advocate. She has earned many of her country's most prestigious literary awards, among them the Jorge Carrera Andrade National Poetry Prize. Her work has been translated into French, English, Hebrew, Portuguese, Swedish and Italian. Quevedo has edited important poetry anthologies, including *13 poetas ecuatorianos nacidos en los 70* (2008) and *De la ligereza o velocidad que también es perfume* (2012). She has also curated the work of other writers with *La música y el Cuerpo: 50 poemas de Eduardo Chirinos* (2015), *Hacer el amor (humor) es difícil pero se aprende*, a selection of stories by Fernando Iwasaki (2014) and, in conjunction with David Curbelo, *Corazón Insular en Mitad del Mundo, 30 poetas cubanos nacidos a partir de 1960 hasta 1985*. She writes for Vallejo&Company, a digital magazine of art and literature.

Among her own poetry collections are: *Cambio en los climas del corazón'* (1989), *La actitud del fuego* (1994), *Algunas rosas verdes* (1996, 2016), *Espacio vacío* (2001, 2008), *Soy mi cuerpo* (2006, 2016), *Dos encendidos* (2008, 2010), *La otra, la misma de Dios* (2011, 2018), *Jardín de dagas* (2014, 2016, 2017); and the anthologies of her poetry: *Música Oscura (*2004), *Amanecer de Fiebre (*2011), *El cielo de mi cuerpo (*2014). Her collected works is titled *Cierta manera de la luz sobre el cuerpo* (2017).

Raspar el tiempo

1

El granizo ha comenzado a disolverse
Hilos helados de agua corren
entre las piedras y las ramas amargas
Parecería que nada se quemó
Que nada fue despojado de su belleza
Tan solo las flores del arupo lucen crispadas
Cristalizadas por tanta pasión del agua
que ha comenzado a disolverse.

2

No es solo la luz que permanece luego de la lluvia
—Un parpadeo—
el olor a barro y tréboles verdes insistiendo
Entre ese parpadeo y la luz
he logrado ver un rostro hermoso
Hacia más de 20 años que no tenía esos ojos frente a los
míos
Si ver llover es tan sencillo
Si desear encontrarme con mi hermano
dependiera de la luz.

3

> *¿Oye alguien mi canción?*
> José Lezama Lima

Ese temblor en las piernas
mirando este paisaje traslúcido

Mar frío y altas rocas
Poca nieve y poco viento para lamentarnos
Sabemos que el deseo
transcurre entre tus manos y el corazón

Destilando cierta bondad desde tus dedos
Ese temblor como escalera al mar
se repite al mirarte a los ojos
¿Oye alguien mi canción?

4

Raspar una hoja larga y verdísima de helecho
Rasparle el tiempo
y su danza constante con las uñas cuadradas
Quitarle el brillo y los diminutos pelitos que la arropan
Raspar sus formas irregulares, fosforecidas y permanentes
Destruirle la belleza al silencio
Pasarle las uñas al tiempo
Pensando en que envejeces dulcemente.

5

Ábreme la puerta
Para que me escape por el cielo límpido
Déjame volar
Y seré una flor en el jardín de la poesía.
Forugh Farrajzad

Sobre la hierba apacible que rodea la casa
distintos modos de derramar pasión
Todos tus yoes sobre la misma hierba
Parte del entramado verde y puntiagudo del espíritu
La vida que se enfrenta con fe y drogas suaves

Distintos modos de vivir en tu apacible casa con la poesía
Cuidar el jardín y volar
De vez en cuando volar . . .
Déjame volar y seré una flor
en el jardín de la poesía.

TO SEARCH TIME

1

The hailstones have begun to dissolve
Frozen threads of water run
between the stones and bitter branches
It seems nothing burned
Nothing lost its beauty
Only the Arupo flowers have contracted
Cristalized by such passion of water
they've begun to disappear

2

It isn't only the light that remains after the rain
—The blink of an eye—
insistent scent of clay and green clover
Between that blink and the light
I have glimpsed a beautiful face
It's been 20 years since my eyes have seen his
If watching the rain were such a simple thing
If only wanting to see my brother
depended on light.

3

> *Does someone hear my song?*
> José Lezama Lima

The trembling in my legs
as I gaze upon that translucent landscape
Cold sea and high rocks

Scant snow and meager wind to make us sad
We know desire
flows between your hands and heart

Distilling a certain kindness in your fingers
That tremor like a ladder to the sea
repeats itself when I look into your eyes
Who hears my song?

4

Scratching a long and intensely green fern leaf
with square fingernails
Scratching time and its constant dance
Removing the glow and tiny hairs they wear
Scratching their irregular shapes, fluorescent and forever
Destroying silence's beauty
Scratching time with my fingernails
Thinking about you sweetly growing old.

5

> *Open the door*
> *So I may escape through pure sky*
> *Let me fly*
> *And I will become a flower in poetry's garden.*
> Forugh Farrajzad

Upon the placid grass around the house
different ways of spreading passion
All your me's are on that grass
It emanates from the spirit's green and piercing web
Life lived with faith and soft drugs

Different ways of living with poetry in your gentle house
To tend the garden and fly
To fly every once in a while . . .
Let me fly and I will become a flower
in poetry's garden.

CORALES

No importa la profundidad del descenso
o la imposible maleza derramada en el camino.
Es largo y frío el viaje sobre oscuros caballos.
Ejercicio de inmersión y belleza piadosa
hasta pisar altos jardines de coral negro.
Entre mi dolor —que conozco tanto desde el lodo—
y el universo poco explorado por la falta de tus palabras,
me quedan flotando la impenetrabilidad de la música y la sal.
Las medusas atrapadas entre mis pestañas me jalan rápido.
Más no importa el precio del descenso.
Es necesario volver al camino consciente del miedo
y el aliento del océano golpeándome en la nuca.

CORAL

The depth of the descent doesn't matter
nor the impossible weeds scattered along the way.
The journey on dark horses is long and cold.
An exercise in immersion and merciful beauty
until we come to high gardens of black coral.
Between my pain —that I know so well from the era of mud—
and the universe I've explored little for lack of your words,
floats the impenetrability of music and salt.
The jellyfish trapped in my eyelashes pull me tight.
And the price of descent matters not.
I must return to the conscious path of fear
and the ocean's breath hitting the nape of my neck.

CARLOS VALLEJO
(1973-)

Carlos Vallejo is from Quito. A photographer as well as a poet, he has won awards in both artistic categories: the Aurelio Espinoza Polit National Literature Prize in 2007, the Ministry of Culture's César Dávila National Literature Prize in 2009, and the first prize in photography awarded by Vanguardia magazine in 2007. In an interview that appeared in Kipus in 2008, Vallejo responded to a question about the nature of poetry in this way: "More than describing the world around us, poetry should express itself at the edges of reality: extending it, planting its foundations where even the outlines of a portrait don't yet exist. Perhaps poetry is that: the pain of borders, the most concrete thrust toward the infinite, as if we were waiting for it to give us an answer, a door, or simply its silence."

Among his poetry collections: *En mi cuerpo no soy libre* (2003), *Fragmento de mar* (2005), *La orilla transparente* (2007), *Oficio de navegantes*, and *Ritual de moscas*. He has a short-story collection titled *Relatos del mal soñar* and is co-author of the book combining poetry and photographs, *Matrioshka*.

CARTA DE MADRUGADA

Fantasma es el tiempo que besas,
beso que se ensancha y no te olvida,
humo pretérito donde hay ascuas,
ascuas que todo lo entienden y no lo dicen.
¿Conoces el relámpago varado en tu distancia?
La semilla del invierno tiembla en mis zapatos.
Oigo el amarillo entre tus pasos,
mas no sé a cuantos palmos de ti transita el amanecer.
Sé de tus mejillas que cruzan blancas
por las horas del desayuno,
y sé de las sombras de tu cielo
llenando los patios.
¿Cuántos calendarios vaciaré este día?,
¿Cómo me sostengo en este solitario sol?
Di más que un siglo, ¡dime más que un ahora!
porque tus labios conocen la fiesta
de nuestros antiguos pájaros.
¿Cuándo vuelves?
Mándame el día. Mándame noticias de tu boca.
Yo te envío un beso,
y dime, en mi comarca, ¿qué perro no te extraña?

DAWN'S LETTER

You kiss a ghostly time,
a kiss that expands and won't let you go,
past-tense smoke where embers remain,
embers that know all and don't let on.
Do you know the lightning stranded in your distance?
A winter's seed trembles in my shoes.
I hear the yellow between your footsteps,
but do not know how far dawn moves past you.
I know your cheeks piercing half-notes
at breakfast time,
and I've heard tell of your sky's shadows
filling courtyards.
How many calendars will I empty today?
How will I stand tall in this solitary sun?
Tell me more than a century, more than a now!
because your lips know the feast
of our ancient birds.
When will you return?
Send me the day. Send me news of your mouth.
I send you a kiss,
and tell me, in my part of the world, what dog doesn't miss
you?

HE CAÍDO DE MUERTE

De vena en vena me voy descolgando,
de raíz en raíz, a latigazos,
por debajo de mi sombra
y de las narices del topo
me despeño, solo,
a lo largo del ojal de mi zapato,
a lo ancho de mis tristes pulgas,
abandono, sin querer, lo inmenso, como huye
esa mancha de luz de la torre vencida,
como se desboca el ingenuo
río perseguido por su vertiente,
caigo, a empellones, a martilladas y codazos,
lluvioso como esa alcantarilla a la que nadie llora;
desciendo de resta en resta
por los centavos del aire,
con mi cuervo en el ojo y mi medio pañuelo,
vencidamente,
a fuerza de gravedad,
cayendo por el hilo de mis silencios,
por el trapecio de la araña
que se desplomó de tedio:
cayendo, por el peso de mis contrincantes,
por el lodo cardíaco y sus decimales;
rasgando el aire entre mis uñas, en picada
por el hueso en polvo y mis oxidados pasos;
asombrado, moribundo, desnudo,
de bruces instalado en mi fila de nadie
para ver este espectáculo de arqueología
en que,
desmoronado de mí, ingenuote,

apunto a fondo las córneas
y me estrello en la vida
como esa bala falsa que disparé frente a mi espejo.

I HAVE FALLEN FROM DEATH

Vein to vein I unleash myself,
from root to root, whipped,
beneath my shadow
and right in the mole's face
I fall, alone,
the length of my shoe's clasp,
breadth of my sad fleas,
without meaning to I abandon greatness,
like that stain of light fleeing from the broken tower,
like the innocent runaway river
pursued by its watershed,
I fall, pummeled by hammers and elbows,
rainy like that gutter no one mourns;
piece by piece I descend
along coins of air,
with a crow in my eye and torn handkerchief,
shattered,
with the force of gravity,
dropped by the thread of my silences,
the trapeze of a spider
collapsing from tedium:
falling, with the weight of my opponents,
with cardiac mud and its decimals;
grasping at the air between my nails, in freefall
by pulverized bone and oxidized steps;
astonished, moribund, naked,
headfirst entrenched in my no one's formation
so that I may view this spectacle of archeology
where,
defeated in myself, great naive one,

I aim my corneas straight ahead
and explode into life
like that make-believe bullet I shot into my mirror.

LUCILA LEMA
(1974-)

Lucila Lema was born in Peguche, Otavalo. She writes in Kichwa (the Quechua dialect that is spoken in Ecuador and Colombia) and translates her work into Spanish. She has worked with indigenous organizations such as the Confederation of Indigenous Nationalities of Ecuador (CONAIE), the Confederation of Indigenous Nationalities of the Eastern Mountain Region (ECUARUNARI), and the Confederation of Peoples of Quechua Nationality (CONFENIAE). CONAIE represents the Shuar, Achuar, Siuona, Secoya, Cofán, Huaorani, Záparo, Chachi Tsáchila, Awá, Epera Manta, Wancavilca and Quechua peoples. Its political agenda includes strengthening a positive indigenous identity, recuperation of land rights, environmental sustainability, opposition to neoliberalism and rejection of US military involvement in South America (such as Plan Colombia). A filmmaker as well as a writer, in 1999 Lema won a prize at the Third Festival of Film and Video of the First Nations of Abya Yalafrom CONAIE for the best video on traditional medicine. In 2000 she won recognition in the Indigenous Woman and Testimonial category for "Publication," and in 2013 she won recognition for photography in the same category at the 1st Continental Biennale of Indigenous Contemporary Arts in Mexico. In 2016 she won the Darío Guevara Mayorga "Rumiñahui de Oro" given by Quito's metropolitan municipal district for the best children's story. She currently teaches literature at the University of the Arts.

Her books are: *Hatun Taki poemas a la madre tierra y a los abuelos* (editor, 2013), *Chawpi pachapi Arawikuna nuestra propia palabra* (editor, 2014), *Ñawpa pachamanta purik rimaykuna Antiguas palabras andantes* (editor, 2016), *Cuento Chaska* (2016), and *Tamyawan Shamukupani* (2019).

From *Tamyawan Shamukupani* (Frag-ments)

3

—tukuyllami kanchik
kanchikrak
kaymi kanchik

mamatapash charirkanchikmi
taytatapash charirkanchiki

paykunami ñukanchik umapi sisa yakuta
sumak tullpu sisakunata churarka
alli kawsayta charipachun nishpa

paykunami
llullu urpikunapa
millay pumakunapa
may illapakunapa
kuyllurkunapa shutikunawan shutichirka

ñukanchik shutikunaka
shuk shuk urkukunapi
shuk shuk rumikunapi
shuk shuk pukyukunapimi

ñukanchik rimayka
mana chinkarina shimikunami kan—
shinami wawakunaman nishka nin Otavalo kuraka taytaka

3

—todo fuimos
todo somos
esto somos

tuvimos madre
tuvimos padre

ellos pusieron sobre nuestras cabezas agua de flores
flores de colores maravillosos
como bienvenida

ellos nos nombraron
con nombres de dulces aves
de feroces pumas
de terrible rayo
de lejana estrella

nuestros nombres
están en cada montaña
en cada piedra
en cada arroyo

nuestros nombres son palabras
para no irnos jamás—
dicen que ha dicho tayta Otavalo a los niños

3

—we were everything
we are everything
this is what we are

we had mother
we had father

they put flower water on our heads
flowers of marvelous colors
to welcome us

they named us
with the names of sweet birds
of ferocious mountain lions
of terrible lightning
of distant star

our names
are on every mountain
on every stone
in every dry river bed

our names are words
to keep us here always—
they say Aunt Otavalo told the children

14

ñuka puriyta mana allikachinakun
yallikta rikushpa
—payka mana kaymantachu nishpa— upallakuta ninakun

kaymanta warmikunaka mana shina tiyarinchu
kaymanta warmikunaka mana shina churakunchu
kaymanta warmikunaka mana shina rimanchu
kaymanta warmikunaka mana yachaywasiman rinchu
kaymanta warmikunaka mana nataka ninchu ninakun

ñukakarin yana urkuta
tunirshka ruku wasita yarikukpipash
ñukanchik kawsakkuna
ñukanchik wañushkakuna chaykunallatak kakpipash

shukmi nishpa rikuwanakun
yallikta rikushpa

—payka mana kaymantachu nishpa— upallakuta ninakun

14

no les gusta mi caminar
me ven pasar y susurran
—ella no es de aquí—

no se sientan así las mujeres de aquí
no se visten así las mujeres de aquí
no hablan así las mujeres de aquí
no van al colegio las mujeres de aquí
no aman a otros hombres las mujeres de aquí
no dicen no las mujeres de aquí

aunque yo extraño el monte negro
y la casa vieja que ahora es tierra
aunque nuestros vivos
y nuestros muertos son los mismos
les parezco extraña
me ven pasar y susurran

—ella no es de aquí—

14

they don't like the way I walk
they see me go by and whisper
—she isn't from here—

she doesn't sit like the women from here
she doesn't dress like the women from here
she doesn't talk like the women from here
the women from here don't go to school
the women from here don't love strange men
the women from here don't say no

although I miss the black mountain
and the old house that has returned to earth
although our living
and our dead are the same
I seem strange to them
they see me go by and whisper

—she isn't from here—

LUIS ALBERTO BRAVO
(1979-)

Luis Alberto Bravo was born in Milagro. He is better known as a novelist and short story writer—for which he has won numerous prizes—but has also produced fine poetry.

His novels are: *Septiembre* (2012), *Hotel Barleby* (2013), *El jardinero de los Rolling Stones* (2015), and *Crow* (2017). His sole book of poetry to date is *Utolands* (2009).

UNA CHICA GOLPEADA EN LA PISCINA

Su lengua ahora es más larga
y hay rastros de pasta dentífrica.

Ahora ella cierra los ojos donde lloraba.

Ahora las hojas vuelan para todos lados,
y vuelven a caer . . .
. . . . cerca de aquí . . .
. . . . . . (Donde estaba la chica golpeada y muerta en la piscina).

La sacaron del agua
como quien saca a un pequeño esqueleto,
como quien carga una madera pintada . . .
O como quien mide al primer amor.

Y mientras le espiaban las nalgas . . .
—*Pero, ¿las nalgas de quien?"*
—*Pues, de ella . . .*
de la chica golpeada y muerta en la piscina"—.
. . . . . . alguien le sacó unas fotos;
Y por ello,
ahora podemos decir cuando nos preguntan
. . . . por la chica golpeada y muerta en la piscina:
. . . . "Ella estaba ahí . . .
. . . . Y nosotros acá . . .
. . . . Y los tipos de las fotos más allá".

En la cercas pintadas
los vecinos murmuran & enrabietados
exclaman: "Si bien, era una mala chica,
no merecía morir en una piscina".

—"Pero, ¿ha muerto quién . . .? ¿Quién ha muerto, quién?
—"Pues ella . . .
La chica golpeada y muerta en la piscina"—.

"Yo le solía traer cervezas,
y cuando me daba propinas
ella solía decir:
.. ..*«Sólo un ángel como yo*
.. ..*dejaría caer sobre ti*
                un pedazo de manzana...
.. ..*—Como quien deja caer sobre una isla—*
.. ..*y verdaderamente lo soy»*
(...) (glup)
Aún así, no tenía que morir en una piscina".

"La mujer de allá,
nos ha dicho que a veces solía verla llorar en el patio,
y luego saltar las cercas pintadas,
sólo para arrancar —con un instrumento del bosque—
todas las manzanas fuertes".

...
Desde aquel día
vengo a esta casa de martes a jueves...
Y siempre, siempre
un pequeño ojo del atardecer
.. .. .perfora las nubes (y luego llueve).
Y entonces... ella abre sus alas, se eleva (y llueve) y abre sus alas
.. .. (como si evocara la luz de un perro sobre una nube

podrida).
—"Pero, ¿quien? ¿Me hablas de quién?"
—"Pues, de ella...
De la chica golpeada y muerta en la piscina"—.

A BEAT-UP GIRL IN THE SWIMMING POOL

Her tongue is longer now
and there is a residue of toothpaste.

Where she cried, now her eyes are closed.

Now leaves fly everywhere,
and fall again . . .
. . . . nearby . . .
. . . . (Where they found the beat-up girl in the
    swimming pool).

They pulled her from the water
as one retrieves a brief skeleton,
as one recovers a piece of painted wood . . .
Or measures first love.

And while they gawked at her buttocks
—*But, whose buttocks?*
—*Well, hers . . .*
the beat-up girl in the swimming pool"—
. . . . someone took some pictures of her;
And so, when they ask, we can say
. . . . the beat-up girl dead in the swimming pool:
. . . ."She was there . . .
. . . . And we were here . . .
. . . . And the guys who took the
pictures over there."

By the painted fences
the neighbors murmur &
exclaim enraged: "Even if she was a bad girl,
she didn't deserve to die in a swimming pool."

—But who died . . .? Who died, who?
—Well her . . .
The beat-up girl in the swimming pool"—

"I used to buy her beer,
and when she tipped me
she'd say:
. . . . *"Only an angel like me*
. . . . *would let a bite of apple*
                fall on you . . .
. . . . *—Like one who lets herself fall on an island—*
. . . . *and I truly am one"*
(. . .) (glup)
Even so, she shouldn't have died in a swimming pool."

"The woman over there,
told us she sometimes saw her crying on the patio,
and then jump the painted fences,
just so she could uproot—with a basic tool—
all the crabapples".

. . .
Ever since that day
I come to this house from Tuesday to Thursday . . .
And always, always
a small eye at evening
. . . . pierces the clouds (and it rains).
And then . . . . she spreads her wings, she rises (and it
rains) and she spreads her wings
. . . . (as if she were conjuring a dog's urge above a
rotten cloud).
—"But, who? Who are you talking about?"
—"Well, her . . .
The girl beat-up and dead in the swimming pool"—.

SANTIAGO GRIJALVA
(1992-)

Santiago Grijalva was born in Ibarra. Recently gradu-
ated from Quito's Universidad Politécnica Salesiana in
Community Social Psychology, he is the head of logistics
and marketing at ElAngel Publishers. Grijalva belongs to
the literary group called Aporema. In 2016 he was an invited
guest at Poesía en Paralelo Cero, and the following year
began working full-time at the festival.

His books of poetry are: *La revolución de tus cuerpos*
(2015), *Arreglos para la historia* (2017), and *Los desperdicios
del polvo* (2018).

DESPEDIDAS PARA NOMBRARTE

Estés en mí como la madera en el palito
Juan Gelman

Los años van en mi contra
me dicen que desvuelva la silueta de los días,
que me esconda en los escondrijos de una memoria
que me enciende
      al sentir como golpean
se enciende,
      se esconde
para que vuelvan a golpear.

Solo suena el cristal
por dentro de la lluvia
solo nace el ayer en las próximas nostalgias,
quedarse sin ser
estar tan cerca de Dios
para sentir su aliento.

Aquí llueve dentro de casa
soles nacen por debajo de la falda del tiempo.
Preguntas por el día
el volver y tu ausencia,
por el fuego de Prometeo,
las espaldas de las tortugas
y por el qué hacer después de nuestro encuentro.

Me voy apagando en esta lluvia
sobre los destellos nacientes del cielo
que cae como un manto oculto en los dedos de la luz,
vuelvo la cabeza
veo agua en mi madera,
rasguños en los dolores y cuerpo.

El fusil aguarda cargado
pero ¿qué queda después de esta guerra?
¿qué después de tanto invierno, de tanto andar errante?

Estás en mi como la madera en el palito
para no soltar la mano fría de mi espera
estoy en ti, como tú
el nosotros en nuestras despedidas.

FAREWELLS TO NAME YOU

You are in me like wood in the plank
Juan Gelman

The years are against me,
they say they're giving back a silhouette of days,
saving me a lair of memory
igniting me
        when I feel their blows,
igniting,
        hiding in fragile order
to evade more blows.

Glass sounds
within rain alone,
yesterday is only born in future nostalgias,
to be here without
getting so close to God
you can feel his breath.

Here it rains inside the house,
suns are born beneath time's skirt.
You ask about the day,
return and your absence,
for Prometheus's fire
the backs of tortoises
and what we must do once we meet.

Here I am burning out in this rain
in the sky's incipient glitter
falling like an unseen blanket on fingers of light,
I turn my head
glimpse water in my wood,
scratches on pain and body.

The gun is kept loaded,
but what remains when this war is over?
After so much winter, so much wandering?

You are in me like wood in the plank
so as not to let go of the cold hand of my waiting
I am in you, like you,
the we in our farewells.

RENÉ GORDILLO (1993)

René Gordillo was born in Ambato. He holds degrees in Communications and Literature from the Pontífica Universidad Católica del Ecuador in Quito. A new voice in Ecuadorian poetry, Gordillo won Paralelo Cero 2019's National Poetry Prize for his book *Poemas de mi patio y de otros lados*. An international jury chose 16 books as finalists out of the 103 submitted. It then awarded first prize to Gordillo. In their decision the three judges wrote: " . . . [his] focus on the patio, garden, domestic space, when our iconic poetry has privileged an open landscape, signals both critique and hope . . . Contemplation has the last word in this book written in a conversational style."

Poemas de mi patio y de otros lados (2019).

POEMA INCOMPLETO

Este es un poema incompleto,
su incompletud me medio llena
el corazón y a duras penas recuerdo
el calor de las piernas de la mujer amada
la otra parte del recuerdo es otra mujer amada.
Y así me acuerdo de media nube, de medio sueño
de la media sonrisa de mi madre, del medio pasaje
en el colegio y la media vista de la ciudad en la media terraza.

El medio mar y la media montaña,
la media aritmética, media de tabacos,
el trabajo a medio tiempo que quise para escribir más y mejor
la media palabra con la que me hubiese resignado para no irme.

Este poema fue hecho con todas las mitades que le faltan,
como todos los poemas es un retazo que no le toca ni el amor
    ni la tristeza
porque son palabras, palabras que si pudieran matarnos de una
vez lo harían.
Pero gracias a Dios, qué bueno esto de escribir la historia de lo
incompleto
para que la nostalgia, si viene, nos tome por partes.

INCOMPLETE POEM

This is an incomplete poem,
its incompleteness fills my heart
halfway and I barely remember
the heat of my beloved's legs,
the other half of that memory belongs to another woman.
And so, I remember half a cloud, half a dream
my mother's half smile, the half landscape
of school and half view of the city from half a balcony.

Half a sea and half a mountain,
half arithmetic, halved cigarettes,
the half-time job I wanted so I could write more and better,
the half a word that would have kept me from leaving.

This poem was made with all the necessary halves,
like all poems it is a remnant untouched by love or sorrow
because it is made of words, words that would kill us
if they could.
But, thank God, it's a good thing to write a history
of the incomplete
so that nostalgia, if it comes, only overcomes us by halves.

JUAN SUAREZ PROAÑO (1993)

Juan Suárez Proaño was born in Otavalo, a highland city known outside Ecuador's borders for its famous indigenous market. He graduated in Communications and Literature from Quito's Pontífica Univesidad Católica. He is part of the organizing committee at Poesía Paralelo Cero.

Nos ha crecido hierba (2018).

ENSEÑANZAS

En la infancia quisieron enseñarnos
el color del cielo
pero jamás nos mostraron
las nubes de humo, no dejaron entrar
el sol de las despedidas.

Nos enseñaron los nombres
y ocultaron su sangre,
aprendimos a deletrear la historia
y repetimos hasta el cansancio
las capitales de la belleza,
los himnos de pájaro exiliado.

Nos enseñaron las palabras de perdón
solo para que pudiéramos repetirlas
cuando amábamos la protección
de la noche.

Nos enseñaron a sumar las culpas
pero nos ocultaron el resultado
de frotar dos rocas
o dos cuerpos
hasta que surja algo.

Nadie nos enseñó
que podían expulsarnos
de dios y de la tierra
si en lugar de decir cuerpo lo mostráramos
si decíamos *mar*
y en el fondo
nos ahogábamos sin preguntas.

Tanto nos enseñaron.

Pero siempre hubo una ventana
que no pudieron tapiar
con años y pizarras:
por esa ventana
entraba a veces
a conversar el mundo.

Teachings

When we were young, they wanted
to teach us the color of the sky
but never showed us
its towers of smoke, didn't include
the sun of its goodbyes.

They taught us names
and hid their blood,
we learned to write history
repeat again and again
those beautiful names of capitals
and the hymns of the exiled bird.

They taught us words of forgiveness
so that we could repeat them
when making love
to night's solace.

They taught us to list our sins
but hid what happens
when two rocks
or two bodies came together
and something new is born.

No one taught us they could expel us
from god and earth
if instead of saying the word *body*
we revealed it,
or said the word *sea*
and drowned unquestioning
in its depths.

They taught us so much.

But there was always a window
they couldn't brick over
with years or blackboards:
through that window
the world sometimes
came to talk.

ABOUT THE EDITOR

Margaret Randall is a feminist poet, writer, photographer and social activist. She is the author of over 150 books. She is the recipient of the 2019 Haydée Santamaría Medal from Casa de las Americas in Havana, and the prestigious 2019 Poeta de Dos Hemisferios, presented by Ecuador's Poesía en Paralelo Cero. In 2017, she was awarded the Medal of Literary Merit by Literatura en el Bravo, Chihuahua, Mexico. The University of New Mexico granted her an honorary doctorate in letters in 2019.

Born in New York City in 1936, she has lived for extended periods in Albuquerque, New York, Seville, Mexico City, Havana, and Managua. Shorter stays in Peru and North Vietnam were also formative. In the 1960s, with Sergio Mondragón she founded and co-edited *El Corno Emplumado / The Plumed Horn,* a bilingual literary journal which for eight years published some of the most dynamic and meaningful writing of an era. Robert Cohen took over when Mondragón left the publication in 1968. From 1984 through 1994 she taught at a number of U.S. universities.

Randall was privileged to live among New York's abstract expressionists in the 1950s and early '60s, participate in the Mexican student movement of 1968, share important years of the Cuban revolution (1969-1980), the first three years of Nicaragua's Sandinista project (1980-1984), and visit North Vietnam during the heroic last months of the U.S. American war in that country (1974). Her four children—Gregory, Sarah, Ximena and Ana—have given her ten grandchildren and two great-grandchildren. She has lived with her life companion, the painter and teacher Barbara Byers, for the past 33 years.

Upon her return to the United States from Nicaragua in 1984, Randall was ordered to be deported when the government invoked the 1952 McCarran-Walter Immigration and Nationality Act, judging opinions expressed in some of her books to be "against the good order and happiness of the United States." The Center for Constitutional Rights defended Randall, and many writers and others joined in an almost five-year battle for reinstatement of citizenship. She won her case in 1989.

In 1990 Randall was awarded the Lillian Hellman and Dashiell Hammett grant for writers victimized by political repression. In 2004 she was the first recipient of PEN New Mexico's Dorothy Doyle Lifetime Achievement Award for Writing and Human Rights Activism.

Recent non-fiction books by Randall include *To Change the World: My Life in Cuba* (Rutgers University Press), *More Than Things* (University of Nebraska Press), *Che On My Mind,* and *Haydée Santamaría, Cuban Revolutionary: She Led by Transgression* (both from Duke University Press). Her most recent nonfiction works are *Only the Road / Solo el Camino: Eight Decades of Cuban Poetry* (Duke University Press, 2016) and *Exporting Revolution: Cuba's Global Solidarity* (Duke University Press, 2017).

"The Unapologetic Life of Margaret Randall" is an hour-long documentary by Minneapolis filmmakers Lu Lippold and Pam Colby. It is distributed by Cinema Guild in New York City.

Randall's most recent collections of poetry and photographs are *Their Backs to the Sea* (2009), *My Town: A Memoir of Albuquerque, New Mexico* (2010), *As If the Empty Chair: Poems for the Disappeared / Como si la silla vacía: poemas para los desaparecidos* (2011), *Where Do We Go from Here?* (2012), *Daughter of Lady Jaguar Shark* (2013), *The Rhizome as a Field of Broken Bones* (2013), *About Little Charlie Lindbergh and other Poems* (2014), *Beneath a Trespass of Sorrow*

(2014), *Bodies / Shields* (2015), *She Becomes Time* (2016), *The Morning After: Poetry and Prose in a Post-Truth World* (2017), and *Against Atrocity* (2019), all published by Wings Press. *Time's Language: Selected Poems (1959-2018)* was published by Wings Press in 2018. Many of Randall's collections of poetry have been published in Spanish translations throughout the hemisphere.

Wings Press was founded in 1975 by Joanie Whitebird and Joseph F. Lomax, both deceased, as "an informal association of artists and cultural mythologists dedicated to the preservation of the literature of the nation of Texas." Publisher, editor and designer since 1995, Bryce Milligan is honored to carry on and expand that mission to include the finest in American writing— meaning all of the Americas, without commercial considerations clouding the decision to publish or not to publish.

Wings Press intends to produce multi-cultural books, chapbooks, ebooks, recordings and broadsides that enlighten the human spirit and enliven the mind. Everyone ever associated with Wings has been or is a writer, and we know well that writing is a transformational art form capable of changing the world, primarily by allowing us to glimpse something of each other's souls. We believe that good writing is innovative, insightful, and interesting. But most of all it is honest. As Bob Dylan put it, "To live outside the law, you must be honest."

Likewise, Wings Press is committed to treating the planet itself as a partner. Thus the press uses as much recycled material as possible, from the paper on which the books are printed to the boxes in which they are shipped.

As Robert Dana wrote in *Against the Grain,* "Small press publishing is personal publishing. In essence, it's a matter of personal vision, personal taste and courage, and personal friendships." Welcome to our world.

COLOPHON

This first edition of *Voices from the Center of the World*, edited by Margaret Randall, has been printed on 55 pound "natural" paper containing a percentage of recycled fiber. Titles have been set in Aquiline Two and Lithos Pro type, the text in Adobe Caslon type. This book was designed by Bryce Milligan.

www.wingspress.com
Wings Press titles are distributed to the trade by the
Independent Publishers Group
www.ipgbook.com
and in Europe by Gazelle
www.gazellebookservices.co.uk

Also available as an ebook.

*For more information about Margaret Randall,
visit her website at www.margaretrandall.org.*